GAME A.I. MADE EASY I: DESIGNING AGENTS

Learn essential concepts and designs in a simplified and beginner-friendly guide.

With examples in C# for Unity3D.

BY RUI JIANG

GAME A.I. MADE EASY I: DESIGNING AGENTS

First edition.

ISBN 9781792608957

This page intentionally left blank.

This page intentionally left blank.

Table of Contents

1 / ABOUT THE GAME A.I. MADE EASY SERIES

Welcome to the **GAME A.I. MADE EASY** series! This is a series of books and educational content aimed at complete beginners or those with limited technical experience who want to realize their creative dreams but feel daunted by the knowledge required to do so.

Instead of calling this another "technical book", we consider this book as part of a larger "course". The books in the series are developed in sequential order in terms of conceptual knowledge and technical difficulty. Therefore, if we consider this book as "Course 1" of the series, it is assumed that you have already learned it when you move onto Book 2 or Course 2.

Book 1 (this book) lays down the essential and fundamental conceptual knowledge that we believe you should learn before moving onto coding or more advanced subjects. Despite having examples in C# and Unity3D engine, this book is not engine-specific or platform-specific. Rather, it provides you with working A.I. designs that you can incorporate into your own games, regardless of the platform. Therefore, you should not expect full-on programming tutorials, but rather, a lightweight reading exercise that will open your mind to the possibilities of game A.I. design. While we do provide coding examples (in C# for Unity3D) to show how certain concepts are put into practice, you're free to skip them.

This book is required learning for you to proceed with Book 2 in the series, where you will learn to create an entire combat A.I. system in Unity3D.

2 /   ABOUT THIS BOOK

2.1 /   WHY LEARN GAME A.I.?

If you're reading this book, then you already know why you are learning A.I. Today, there are thousands of high quality games on Steam and millions more on the Android and iOS app stores.   The current market is divided between AAA studios and lower budget independent (indie) developers. Even some indie-developers are actually former employees of AAA game companies and have ample experience under their belts. Other successful game developers are the AAA studios themselves that hire entire teams of artists and A.I. programmers. Thus it's natural for industry newcomers to feel daunted by the competition. You may have paid for online tutorials and learned the tools but still have no idea of where to begin in terms of creating A.I. – a critical element to many successful games. A.I. agents that are realistically convincing can either make or break a game upon its release. Therefore, it's imperative that game developers and designers become familiar with the techniques for creating captivating game A.I. But worry not! With this book and the growing popularity of low-cost AAA game engines such as Unity3D, Unreal, and CryEngine, you have a chance to compete – and a great chance at that.

2.2 /   THE GOALS OF THIS BOOK

This book's primary goal is to teach you how to *think* in the art of A.I. for games and how to *design* them. It is not a collection of programming tutorials (check out Book 2 in the series where you learn to build an entire combat A.I. system in Unity3D). This book seeks to empower complete beginners or those with limited programming experience to design interesting A.I. characters for their games that can compete in the ever-growing market today. This book is meant to be an easy-read and easy to digest for those with a light technical background.

2.3 /   MAKING IT EASY

This book breaks down difficult, and often convoluted concepts in gaming A.I. and presents them in a clear and easy-to-understand manner. It squeezes out the pulp of complex theories and abstract concepts in computer science to serve you just the juice that matters for developing a high quality game – advice that is practical and essential. You need not understand Markov decision processes, naive Bayes, Fibonacci heaps, or heuristics, or even know that such words exist, to create professional A.I. for gaming. Using this book, some creativity, and the right tools, you too can create challenging characters for additive gaming experiences.

This book aims to provide you with easy-to-understand explanations for A.I. concepts, inspiration for character design, and blueprints for designing interesting virtual agents – blueprints that we hope our readers will frequently will refer back to during their game development careers. This book contains very little source code, as we do not wish to restrict our designs to a single system or programming language. Further, many game development tools available today do not require the developer to write a single line of code. Finally, we wrote this book for you, in the hopes that it will be an easy, informative, and potentially career-changing read.

Each chapter is powered by the philosophy that one does not need a background in A.I. fields such as machine learning or neural networks to develop A.I. for games. In fact, as we will explain in later chapters, you may be relieved to learn that most of the A.I. used in video games today should not be considered as "real A.I." at all. Instead, they are often rule-based simulations of intelligence to give the illusion of artificial intelligence. In video game design, we are mostly concerned with the art of "illusion" and game A.I. programming is no exception, for we are usually only required to *simulate* or to give the appearance of intelligence in virtual characters. **Therefore, the barriers to entry for newbie game developers is much lower than what you had probably expected.**

2.4 /   A DESIGN GUIDE

Our secondary objective in creating this book was to provide a reference guide – a "playbook", if you will – for experienced developers to come back to for design ideas and blueprints. Again, this works well with the fact that we made the book platform-independent and programming-language independent. We hope our designs will inspire and guide you throughout all phases of development.

We begin with a general introduction to gaming A.I. and decision trees. Afterwards, you will be introduced modular A.I. design – our model for designing A.I. systems that are organized, robust, simple to modify, and high performance. We will build on this modular concept by detailing each module, their functions and relationships with each other. You will be introduced to pathfinding, a technical area that is often difficult to understand for those without a computer science background. We will cover A.I. tactics such as stealth operations, flanking, squad formations, and more. We then introduce you to simple adaptive A.I. and their advantages and disadvantages. Afterwards, we put it all together by designing a central "brain" that combines all of these modules to create a Finite State Machine that defines the A.I. character. And finally, we provide examples of A.I. designs and usage in popular game genres and multiplayer considerations.

2.5 /   WHO THIS BOOK IS FOR

- Complete beginners to both game development and game A.I.

- People who have watched many video tutorials (Unity3D, Unreal, CryEngine, etc) and read the documentations but are still uncertain about many areas of game development or where to begin in terms of building A.I.

- People with no coding experience who want an easy-to-read introduction to game A.I (such people can skip the coding sections).

- People with some programming experience but have no idea where to begin in designing A.I. for games.

- Artists that do not come from a computer science background, but would like to be able to develop intelligent agents for their dream game.

- Developers who have already published a few games and would like additional guidance in designing A.I.

- Experienced programmers who want to break into game development as quickly as possible.

- Anyone looking for some inspiration in designing their A.I. characters.

3 /   REQUIREMENTS

If you're using this book for a quick read, as an introduction to game A.I. design, then nothing else is required of you – only your willingness to learn new ideas!

If you're looking to apply the ideas, decision trees, and designs presented in this book, you will need to have a basic understanding of the tools you will be using. For example, if you're using light Javascript game frameworks, or the heavier Unity3D, Unreal Engine, or CryEngine/Lumberyard tools, you'll need a basic understanding of the coordinate system, Vectors, how to make an object move across the scene, how to set up animations, import models, and create variables to hold data such as numbers and strings.

This book was written with the assumption that some readers will be using tools that require no coding at all, while others will be scripting their games. The ideas presented in this book are meant for developers in both cases.

In providing examples, this book uses the Unity3D game engine (code compatible with versions 2017 and beyond). As a result, a few concepts may differ from the other engines. For example, a difference between Unity and Unreal Engine is that the X and Z coordinate system is reversed. When we discuss a position with X, we mean the X position for Unity, which may differ from that of another engine. To minimize confusion, we usually preface an example using universal terms, such as "forward vector", which represents the same concept in both Unity 3D and Unreal Engine but differs in execution (X and Z positions are switched).

4 / INTRODUCTION TO GAME A.I.

4.1 / DEFINING "ARTIFICIAL INTELLIGENCE"

Before we move into applied artificial intelligence in game development, we must first understand what **artificial intelligence** (A.I.) is. Depending on who you ask, an exact definition of "artificial intelligence" may vary but the study of A.I. is, broadly speaking, the **study of intelligent entities**. Specifically, artificial intelligence involves **perception (sensory)** and **actions**. We'll touch on each of these later.

4.2 / DEFINING "AGENTS"

In the field of A.I., the term **"agent"** refers to anything that has perception and the capability to take action. In game development, we also call them **"NPCs"**, short for **non-player character**. In this book, we use "agent" and "NPC" interchangeably. A real life example of an agent can be an autonomous car. Here, the agent receives data about its environment using its **perception** system, a plethora of sensors, cameras, and a GPS to detect road obstacles and to find a path to its destination. Based on this perception data, the agent can decide to take **actions**, such as evading obstacles, auto-braking, turning, and adjusting cruising speed.

As another example, and one that is most relevant to us, an agent can be a virtual character inside a video game that has perception (awareness about its environment, in this case, the game level) and acts (move around, shoot at targets) on that perception. This type of agent is usually visually represented by a 2D or 3D graphical avatar, often enhanced with animations and audio playback.

As you can see, the term "agent" in the field of AI can refer to either intelligent entities in real life or in a virtual environment. This book strictly deals with virtual agents. Most of the techniques presented in this book are incompatible with agents in real life (e.g., robotics) due to the complexity of real life environments. For example, even in the most extreme cases of randomly or procedurally generated video game environments, a virtual agent can still quickly map out the entire level, storing every bit of position data of all obstacles, enemies, and objectives in its memory, and move towards objectives flawlessly, avoiding obstacles during transit. This is because once the virtual game environment finishes loading on a player's computer, the A.I. engine has access to a complete virtual "picture" of the entire game level and all it has to do is lookup the position coordinates of a specific object. On the other hand, a real life robot that is attempting to navigate a parking lot filled with cars and obstacles will have much more trouble because it is difficult to obtain live access to a bird's eye view of that environment. There are simply too many factors to consider, from stationary cars, to unpredictable pedestrians, to even the weather (e.g. what happens when the robot moves into a puddle during heavy rain?). Some of today's leading machine learning researchers and A.I. companies specializing in autonomous cars are working to find reliable solutions in the areas touched by the latter example. While "agent" can refer to either virtual or real life A.I., there are differences between designing gaming agents and agents that are really built upon the theoretical foundations of artificial intelligence, such as advanced robotics or complex A.I. applications, which brings us to the next topic...

4.3 /   IS GAME A.I. CONSIDERED "REAL" A.I.?

During the course of your game development career, you may encounter the debate on whether agents in video games count as exhibiting real "artificial intelligence." While non-player characters in video games have long been lumped together and generalized as "A.I." by developers and gamers alike, some academics in the A.I. field argue that video game agents are not real A.I.

The video game industry enjoys a long history of utilizing research in artificial intelligence to power virtual characters. In 1968, three A.I. scientists at the Stanford Research Institute created the A-Star pathfinding algorithm employed by a robot to move around a room. This gave way to the first autonomous machines. Today, that same A-Star algorithm is widely used in video game development to power moving agents, especially in first person shooters, racing games, and real time strategy war games. In the realm of chess, tree-search algorithms were utilized to build powerful virtual chess opponents. More recently, Google's Deep Mind project entered into a partnership with the Blizzard game company to use their popular game Starcraft 2 for academic A.I. research. Clearly, there are mutual benefits when the video game industry and the A.I. research community cross paths.

While some algorithms and techniques created from the A.I. research community are prevalent in video games today, we feel that not all virtual agents should be considered "real" A.I. And in the most popular games today, they're not. Often, a virtual agent is simply following a straightforward set of rules to give the *appearance* that it exhibits some level of intelligence (e.g., *if the light turns green, move forward; otherwise, stop* – this behavior is not A.I., but just a set of coded rules). Even in some AAA-level games that house complex virtual characters that can walk, eat, sleep, follow the player around, and simulate human-like emotions, such virtual agents are simply just following a series of conditional rules that can be easily implemented by most programmers without any background in A.I. For example, imagine a townsman that lives inside a virtual town in a complex role-playing game. This townsman will eat when hungry and sleep when tired. A programmer can easily implement this by simply using variables to represent "hunger" and "strength". This townsman's hunger and strength levels can begin at 100 and drop by 1 every other minute. This agent can simply run through a series of conditional rules (e.g. is "hunger" below 50? is "strength" below 25?) to decide whether to trigger an "eat" or "sleep" action. In the event that this agent's "hunger" level is at 38 (below 50), two major functions will be triggered: The first tells the agent to move towards the "kitchen" area and the second triggers the agent's animation module to play an eating animation (animations are usually created by a 3D artist on the dev team and integrated into the game by a programmer). In this example, the agent is not considered to be "real" A.I., but rather, a virtual simulation of what appears to be an intelligent entity.

One of the reasons that some A.I. scientists do not consider game A.I. to be real A.I. involves the ultimate goals of game A.I. and the field of A.I. research. Generally, A.I. researchers work to develop intelligent agents that perfectly accomplish their given tasks and "rational" agents that always select the perfect solutions and actions. In military research, this can be a drone that seeks to absolutely destroy its target. In the autonomous vehicle industry, this can be a self-driving car that must always keep its passengers safe while finding the optimal path to its destination. **In the gaming industry, however, an agent's ultimate objective is not to cause defeat, but to *maximize pleasure* for the human player.** This critical distinction between the ultimate objectives of real academic A.I. and game A.I. must be considered when designing a captivating game, a distinction we must cover next.

4.4 /   THE ULTIMATE OBJECTIVE OF GAME A.I.

The primary objective of game A.I. is not absolute victory, but absolute pleasure for the human player. So that you will remember it, this book will often repeat this thinking: that the ultimate goal of a video game agent is to help the game designer maximize the enjoyment and satisfaction of his end user, a human player. Thus, a video game agent should not seek to always play perfectly or to defeat a human opponent. Rather, the game agent should play at a difficulty against its human opponent that perfectly balances being a challenge with providing pleasure. Human players understand and can feel the discouraging emotions caused by frustration; machines cannot. A player that become repeatedly frustrated by an agent that is too powerful to defeat will most likely never play the game again. On the other hand, a virtual opponent that is too easy or predictable will easily bore them. When designing and developing virtual agents, you must constantly seek that balance between agents your players will describe as "too easy" or "too stupid" and agents that are "too tough" or "too Godly." (these are common phrases taken from gamer reviews on popular market sites). A good mindset to have is to imagine your virtual characters as *actors* on a stage whose full time jobs are to entertain their human audience, that is, to engender tension, provoke emotional responses such as laughter or sadness, instead of working against its audience as powerful, armor-clad giants bent on absolute victory.

5 /   INTRODUCTION TO DECISION TREES

Decision trees are crucial to game A.I. development and we use them quite often in this book. Thus, it is important to become familiar with them early on.

A decision tree simply helps an A.I. agent to decide the right course of action, given certain conditions and events. The "tree" in "decision tree" simply means that the thinking process is made up of many branches of events, actions, and conditions.   For example, consider this game scenario:

An A.I. agent is guarding a gate and notices that someone is approaching. This agent thinks to himself:

(A) Is an unidentified agent approaching my gate?

(B) **[Answer: YES]**. Ok. Is he friend or foe?

(C) **[Answer: FOE]** Ok. Do I have an available and activated weapon?

(D) **[Answer: YES]** Ok. Is enemy agent within my attack distance?

(E) **[Answer: NO]** Ok. I should wait for my target to come close. Go back to **[STEP D] (loop)**

(F) How about now? Is my target within my shooting range?

(G) **[Answer: YES]** Ok. I will play the animation to make my arm raise the rifle.

(H) **[Action: ANIMATION PLAYS]** Ok. Now I will attack...

(I) **[Action: I FIRE MY WEAPON]** Ok. Did I hit my target?

(J) **[Answer: YES]** Ok. Did I kill my target?

(K) **[Answer: YES]** Ok. I should lower my rifle and go back to **[STEP A] (loop)**

This is a very simple example of an A.I. agent using a decision tree with looping procedures to decide whether to fire his weapon, a simplified version of the thought process of a guard in real life. Each lettered step (A, B, C...) branches out to another, depending on which conditions are met. Finally, when the A.I. reaches the terminating condition (STEP K), it will loop back to the beginning (STEP A), and stand guard again, in case another enemy shows up. It's important to note that in this simple example, we left out all the negating conditions for brevity purposes. If this were an actual decision tree, there would be multiple branches stemming out from each step. For example, STEP A would branch out to STEP B [Yes] and also to an additional step [NO], where the A.I. will take action if the unknown agent was a friendly.

SIMPLE DECISION TREE EXAMPLE

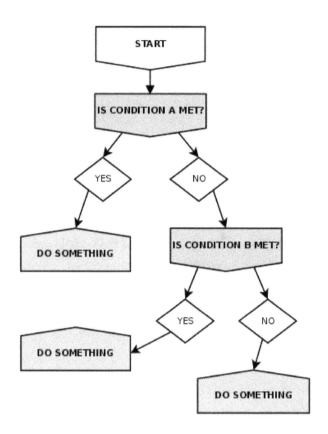

If you're a coder, you can apply this concept to your scripts with the help of if-then statements, loops, and finite state machines (more on that later). If you're a non-coder, you can use visual-programming tools to draw out a similar diagram like the one above. Regardless of the visual system you use (PlayMaker for Unity3D, Unreal Engine's Blueprints, or some other tool), the concept of branches between events, conditions, and actions are the same. The tools will automatically generate the code necessary to implement the design. We will be using decision tree diagrams like this one often throughout the book.

6 / DESIGNING A MODULAR SYSTEM

All of the A.I. designs presented in this book share the common, underlying core concept of **modularity,** that is, designs that comprise multiple organs, each with specific and unique functions, working together in an organized fashion. In our case, multiple modules – A.I. vision, combat, movement, and more – work together to power a single A.I. agent.   Thus, it's important that you understand what modularity is, how it affects you, the developer, and why it is beneficial to the A.I. design and development processes.

In the context of our A.I. designs, a "module" is simply a collection of code or elements with specific functions. This collection of code can communicate with other collections of code and they work together to form an A.I. agent. For example, one collection of code may only deal with counting the A.I. remaining health. Another collection of code may only concern moving the A.I., pixel by pixel, across the screen. Each collection of code only concerns a limited amount of functionality, so that it can be duplicated and re-used for other A.I. types. But you might wonder how such a design scheme may be beneficial to you, the developer. If you're already familiar with object-oriented programming, or designing a program using classes, you already know the benefits of modularity. But how and why should that apply to game A.I. design?

Imagine you are an astronaut in space, living in a space shuttle where every core function is glued into one piece, so that the main engine also powers the life support system, which also powers the shuttle doors. In this case, there are no separate components, but one single component that does everything. If the shuttle engine fails, so would life support, and the shuttle doors would stay sealed shut. Similarly if the life support functions began shutting down, so would the shuttle doors and engine, giving you no means of escaping. Now, suppose the engine failed and your crew decided to conduct repairs on such a system. Where would you even start such repairs? Since everything is glued as one giant singular component, repairing one part may break another. By opening up and repairing the engine, you risk damaging the life support. Perhaps even to get to the engine, you must bypass or break apart the life support or other functions blocking your way. This design is a jungle of titanic mess. If this were a complex video game, it would be near impossible to patch updates to the code or even complete the project on time.

Perhaps we can upgrade our shuttle design with a modular approach. Much like your car, we can slice up each major function and place them in their own compartments. Each compartment, or module, would then be linked to one another or to a central core computer. This way, conducting repairs on the shuttle engine would not risk damage to the life support or door operations. And as a bonus, it would also be possible to switch out or upgrade the engine in the future, without having to upgrade the other components.

In the case of A.I. design, the shuttle metaphor is the virtual agent that your player, the end user, interacts with. Your end user does not care about the approach you took to create that character, only that it allows him to enjoy a pleasurable gaming experience. However, for you, the developer, a non-modular approach can mean a world of difference. A non-modular A.I. system means that you could spend months taking apart your code just to add new functionality, and additional weeks fixing it when your new functionality breaks your existing A.I. scripts. If you want to adjust a function, swap it with another, or duplicate a function to create a new character, it can quickly become messy, time consuming, and exhausting. Meanwhile, a modular A.I. system allows you to swap out A.I. behaviors, build new functionality without breaking existing ones, and easily re-use modules to create new characters.

This simple shuttle example shows the kinds of consequences that arise when your A.I. designs are not modular. Imagining this scenario and planning in a modular context is the kind of thinking you should have when designing your A.I. systems.

Assume you are developing a game that requires 3 unique combat units: A soldier, a medic, and a tank. Each unit has the ability to take damage, move around the map, identify enemies, and receive commands from the player. Some units will be able to fire weapons, and others will have the ability to heal teammates. Taking a modular approach, you first create a Health Module that can take damage from weapons. Next, you create a Movement module that gives an object the ability to move around your map. And finally, you create an Awareness module that can identify and detect nearby enemies. You then connect all 3 modules (Health + Movement + Perception/Awareness) to create a very basic A.I. character that can move around the map and alert you to nearby enemies. Perhaps this can serve as the base for a civilian character without combat capabilities.

Moving on, you create a new module and call it the Combat module. The combat module gives an object the ability to load a variety of weapons and fire them. So now you combine all 4 modules (Health + Movement + Perception + Combat) to create your first unit, the Soldier. You make some adjustments to this unit's endurance

(Health module), run speed (Movement module), and the type of weapon he uses (Combat module).

It now becomes simple to create your next unit, the Tank. Without having to write new code, you simply make a copy of all 4 modules used in the Soldier unit. You combine all 4 modules (Health + Movement + Perception + Combat) and make some adjustments – more health, less movement speed, bigger weapon – to create your new unit.

For your final unit, the Medic, you create a new module and call it the Healing module. You simple connect this new module to copies of the 4 previous modules, make some adjustments to the variables, and you will have created a new Medic unit without having to re-write a single line of code.

Designing A.I. in a modular context gives you many benefits. As you will see, the A.I. designs in the rest of this book are powered by the core principle of modularity.

7 /   SIMPLE MODULAR A.I. CONCEPT

Now that you are familiar with modular design, here is an example of a modular agent. We will go into detail about each module later in the book, in their respective chapters.

The following diagram represents an A.I. character that has a unique identity, can see and identify enemies, be killed, engage in combat, move across the scene, and play animations. Each module (Identity, Awareness, Health, Combat, Movement, Death Effects, and Animation) has its own purpose and unique function area. These modules work independently but can communicate with one another, such as the Combat module's ability to trigger the Animation module to play an attack animation. These modules are all controlled by a Central Brain Module, which makes decisions based on data collected from the other modules.

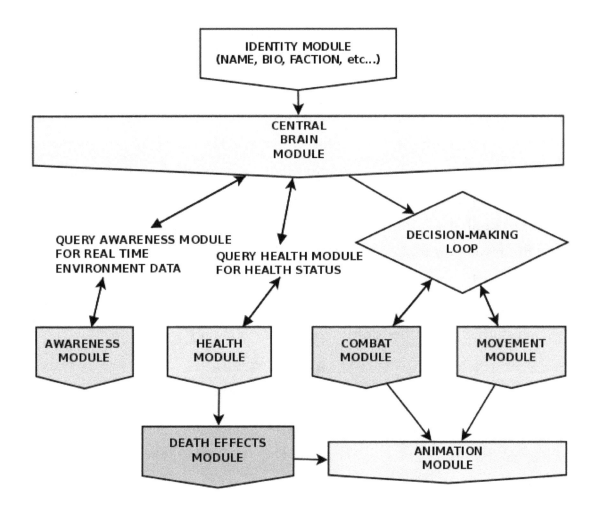

A good way of picturing how these modules work, is the human body. A human's hands have the unique function of grabbing objects. The legs provide balance and the capability to move the body across distances. The eyes, ears, and nose all have unique functions for receiving data about the environment they're in. But the hands will not automatically grab an object if the central brain doesn't tell them to. Legs will not move the body if the brain doesn't send them the message. And the eyes, ears, and nose won't have much use if the data they received (light, color, sound, and smell) did not have a central brain to process it. So, much like the human body, our modular A.I. system is composed of many modules and tied together by a central brain.

To apply this model to our A.I. programming, each module represents a collection of code that provide capabilities in specific areas, with a central brain tying them all together. At the most basic level, this central brain module is simply a system of inputs and outputs. It's a collection of code that triggers specific functions in the modules, receives data back, and then triggers more functions in other modules. For example, in the diagram above, the Central Brain asks for data from the Awareness module, which is continuously gathering information about nearby enemies and their distance to the agent. If the Central Brain receives data that a nearby enemy is within 10 feet of itself, it will trigger the Combat module to fire a weapon. In addition, the Central Brain will also trigger the Movement module to run towards the enemy. Consequently, the Movement module will trigger the Animation module to play the character's running animation. As all this is happening, the Awareness module continues, undisturbed, to gather data about its surrounding area.

This next diagram shows our simple modular A.I. in more detail.

(See diagram on next page)

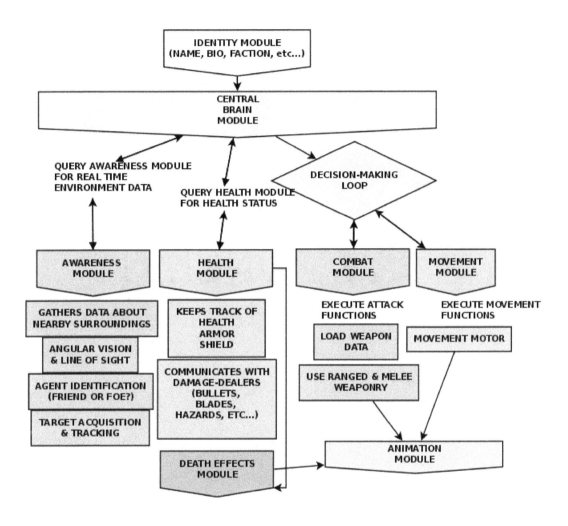

Each module has specific functions unique to its area. The proper organization of specific function groups is crucial to creating high quality, efficient, and robust A.I. systems.

In the next chapter, we will expand on this design to create a more advanced A.I. agent.

8 /   ADVANCED MODULAR A.I. CONCEPT

In this chapter, we expand on our previous design with the addition of more modules.

The new Signals module gives the agent the means to send and receive data from other agents and human players. For example, the agent might send a request for backup, or receive a command from the human player to move to a specific location.

We added a Speech module that gives agent dialogue capabilities to simulate communication with the human player. In Role Playing games, this module is typically used to display multiple dialogue options and replies to the player.

The new Patrol & Wander module allows the agent to patrol along a predefined route, or to dynamically generate a random route. In some games, this module can power a palace guard to patrol a castle's premises, or wild deer to randomly roam the forest.

The Tactics module gives tactical capabilities to the agent, including sending and responding to backup calls, flanking targets, squad formations, and more. It can communicate with the Movement module to move the agent to the desired location, such as its place in a squad formation, or an area near its target's flank.

The Noise module emits noise data when the agent takes specific actions. For example, the Movement module might communicate with this Noise module and trigger a noise level of 50. If a nearby agent's Awareness module can detect noise of at least 50 within its radius, then it will be alerted to this agent.

The Inventory module stores an array of data about weapons, props, and other objects. Additionally, it keeps track of the quantity of objects remaining, such as ammo. Other modules, particularly the Combat module, can query the Inventory about the quantity of remaining ammo, and make the decision of whether it can continue firing its weapon. The next page shows a more detailed diagram of the advanced A.I. module.

The following diagrams show an overview and details of the advanced modules.

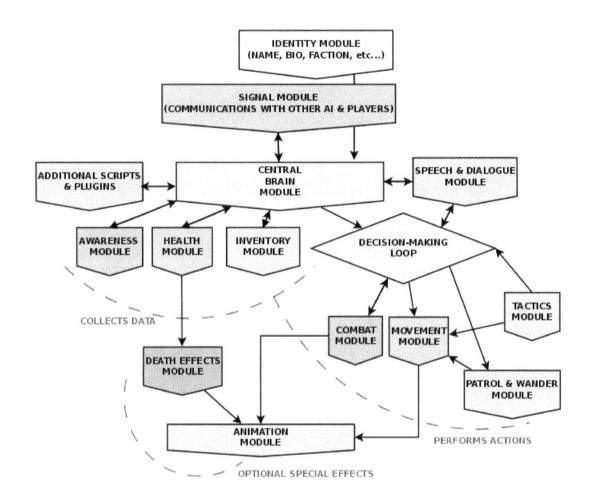

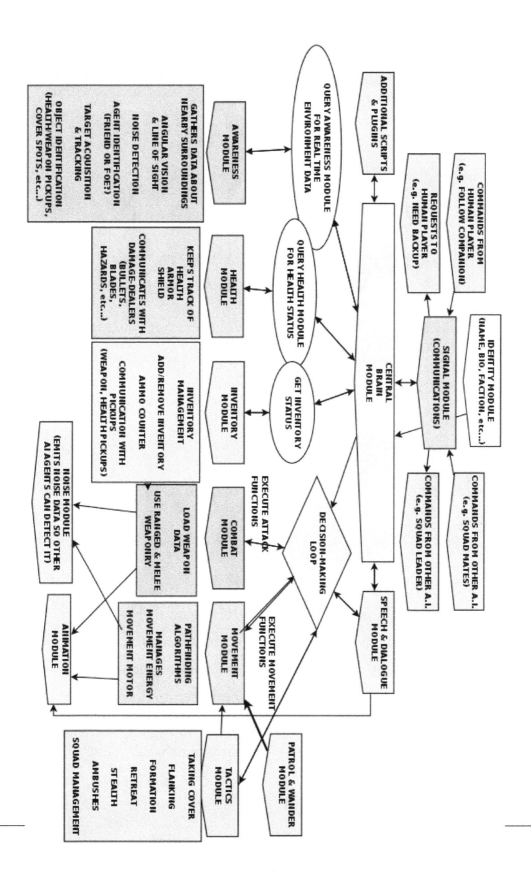

9 /   "ZONES" & UNPREDICTABILITY

9.1 /   DEFINING "ZONES"

In this book, the term "zone" is used quite often, and while you may not encounter the exact vocabulary when working on game projects, the concept is frequent in game A.I. design, particularly in the areas of tactics and movement. This concept is quite simple: A zone is a clearly defined area that can be any shape or form. A fence system around a house is a zone. The restricted area inside a power plant is a zone. The area that a guard patrols around a bank is a zone, specifically, a patrol zone. Zones can be beneficial to game A.I., including helping to define an agent's vision area, and creating unpredictable A.I. by establishing an area in which an agent may randomly move around.

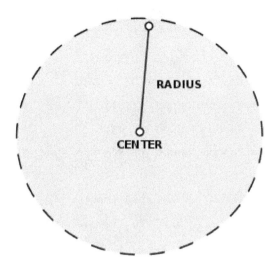

9.2 /   CREATING A ZONE PROGRAMATICALLY

In a virtual environment, a zone is defined by an area established around a center point and a radius (distance from center point to edge). Zones can be represented in programming simply by defining the minimum and maximum coordinates of an area using variables.   In the Unity 3D engine, a zone can be created using two variables:

```
// the following 2 variables will be used to define a radial zone at
// center point 'c'  with an area size created by radius 'r'
Vector3 c = new Vector3(0, 0, 0);
float r = 5;
```

Note that there is no function to actually *create* this zone. The zone is implied when an agent selects a position inside of it. For example, to select a random point inside a 3D spherical zone, we would use code similar to the following:

```
// the following 2 variables will be used to define a radial zone at
// center point 'c'  with an area size created by radius 'r'
Vector3 c = new Vector3(0, 0, 0);
float r = 5;


public void PickRandomPointInZone(){
   float randomX = Random.Range(-r, r);
   float randomY = Random.Range(-r, r);
   float randomZ = Random.Range(-r, r);


   Vector3 randomPoint = new Vector3 (center.x + randomX, center.y + randomY,
         center.z + randomZ);


}
```

The above code will give the variable *randomPoint* a random point inside of the spherical zone defined by c and r. If this had been implemented on an airborne agent, such as a fighter jet in a dogfight sim, the jet will receive a 360-degree position (*randomPoint*) to rotate towards. But what if your agent is not an airborne agent and should not have 360-degrees of freedom of rotational movement?   To simulate a humanoid-like agent that can only rotate 180 degrees we will use the same method but with a simple modification: Keep the Y (height) position constant.

```
// the following 2 variables will be used to define a radial zone at
// center point 'c'  with an area size created by radius 'r'
Vector3 c = new Vector3(0, 0, 0);
float r = 5;


public void PickRandomPointInZone(){
   float randomX = Random.Range(-r, r);
   float randomY = Random.Range(-r, r); // we won't use this time
   float randomZ = Random.Range(-r, r);
```

```
Vector3 randomPoint = new Vector3 (center.x + randomX, center.y,
        center.z + randomZ); }
```

9.3 /   CHECK IF AN OBJECT IS INSIDE A ZONE

To check if a game object is within a zone defined by a center c and radius r, we perform the following two steps:

1.   Find the distance between the object's position and the center of the zone.

2.   Check if that distance is less than or equal to the radius.

In Unity, we can do this programatically:

```
// the following 2 variables will be used to define a radial zone
Vector3 c = new Vector3(0, 0, 0);
float r = 5;
Transform targetObject;


function CheckIfObjectInsideZone(){
   if (Vector3.Distance(targetObject.position, c) <= r) {
        Debug.Log ("Object is inside the zone");
   } else {
        Debug.Log ("Object is outside the zone");
   }
}
```

Zones can be used by agents to gather information about its surrounding area. For example, a zone of vision of 50 radius may allow the A.I. to identify hostiles across a distance of 50 units. Furthermore, a blind zone of 25 radius behind the A.I. can tell hostile agents that moving within that zone will render him undetectable.

9.4 /   REDUCING PREDICABILITY

Zones are also important in creating interesting A.I. agents that are not predictable. Instead of giving an agent an exact position to move to, you can instruct him to move into a zone instead, in which he will pick a random spot. For example, instead of instructing an A.I. enemy to always run to the green car, you can instruct him to move to a small area *around* the green car, randomly. In this case, while your player may expect the agent to move *near* the car, he cannot predict the exact point he will end up. This creates an unpredictable agent.

To better illustrate this, let's assume a hypothetical real life scenario involving your mailbox, the mailman, and your evil neighbor Larry. Every day, the mailman arrives at the same exact location of your mailbox to deliver your mail. And every day, for the last 100 days, you've walked to that same exact location to pick up your mail. Evil Larry, for sinister purposes, had been secretly observing you. He notes that you have used the exact same path to the mail box, 100 out of 100 days. Because of that, he can predict with 99% certainty the path you will take from your door to the mailbox for future dates. That is called predictability and it makes for a boring gaming experience, not to mention greatly reducing your game's replay value.

But imagine that, instead placing your mailbox at a predetermined spot, you install a large fence around your front lawn. This fence forms a large circular shape. You place a large sign on the fence that reads "TOSS MAIL HERE". Now, when the mailman comes by, he throws your mail into the air and over the fence, each package landing at a random position inside your fence. Here, the situation becomes more interesting. Evil Larry can no longer predict the exact path you will take. He can only predict that you will be *somewhere* inside the fence zone, but never *exactly where*. If your neighbor is a player in your game, this circumstance will force him to be more focused, change his tactics frequently, and on the edge of his seat.

For the rest of the book, whenever I mention "zone", I will be referring to a radial zone with a dynamic center point and predetermined radius.

10 / TUTORIAL: QUICK UNITY SETUP

10.1 / INTRODUCTION

While this book mainly deals with concepts and designs, and keeps coding tutorials to a minimum, there are cases where it would help to show you how certain designs are applied in practice. The coding examples assume that you already know the basic concepts of Unity, such as prefabs, gameobjects, tweaking parameters in the Unity Inspector, mechanim animation, etc. It also assumes you have a beginner's knowledge of C#. **Note: This book is mainly unconcerned with programming. For an extensive C# coding tutorial, please check out Book 2 of this GAME AI MADE EASY series where you'll learn to build an entire A.I. system in Unity3D.**

\

We will first make a quick scene setup in Unity3D. Please create a new blank project and follow this tutorial. **If you're not interested in the coding examples, you may skip this chapter.**

10.2 /   TUTORIAL: THE SETUP

Open up Unity and create a new project. Name it anything you'd like.

Unity will start with the default blank scene. Save this scene as "Tutorial 1".

We need to create a basic environment for our agents to live in.
So create a Plane object at the center of the scene (0, 0, 0):

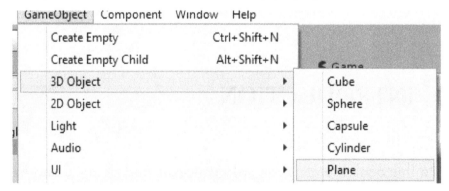

Rename the Plane object to "Ground". From now on, we will refer to this object as Ground.

Our simple scene should look something like this:

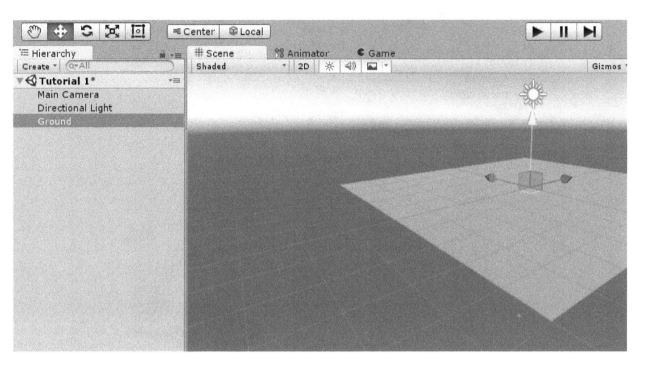

However, this area is a bit small for the AI to move in. So for our purposes, we're going to make it big enough for our agents to roam around.   Set the Scale of Ground to (50, 1, 50):

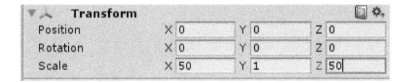

Now we'll create a simple representation of our Agent. Insert a Capsule into the scene and rename it "Agent":

Save the scene. In the next chapter, we will begin creating our AI system by coding our first module.

11 / IDENTITY SYSTEM

11.1 / INTRODUCTION

The Identity module should be a simple, resource-light collection of variables that help give each individual A.I. agent its unique identity. AI can use the Identity component to identify each other and human players can use this to identify characters or factions during gameplay.

Biographical

Variables such as "Name", "Home Planet", "Gender", "Character Lore" and other information that helps to create a more immersive atmosphere for your players.

Faction

Faction tags, such as "Team1", "Team2", "Human Alliance", or "Martian Rebels" define the teams and organizations to which an agent belongs. Additionally, agents will use the faction tags of other agents to distinguish between friend or foe.

Art and Audio

The Identity module may also contain references to art and sound assets such as character portraits and dialogue.

Random Generation

A list of possible random names, birth places, and factions can be stored on the agent so that the agent instantiates with randomly-generated biographies at runtime.

Represented programmatically, the Identity module can simply be a Class or script with a collection of global variable declarations that can be used at runtime.

11.2 /   TUTORIAL: THE SETUP

Create a new folder in our Assets/ folder named "Scripts":

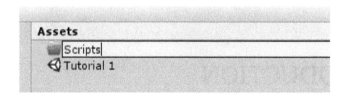

Go into the new folder and right-click inside for a menu. Click Create → New C# Script:

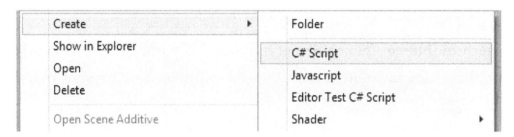

Rename the script as "Identity.cs":

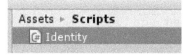

Open the script in your editor.

Delete the default *Start()* and *Update()* methods.

11.3 /   TUTORIAL: THE CODE

```
using UnityEngine;
using System.Collections;


public class Identity : MonoBehaviour {

   public string charName = "Unnamed AI";
   public string bio = "This character's past is shrouded in mystery...";
   public string charClass = "Assault";
   public int age = 35;
   public string race = "Human";
   public string gender = "Male";
   public string[] otherInfo;


}
```

Save the script.

Finally, click our Agent object in the scene and attach this component we just created:

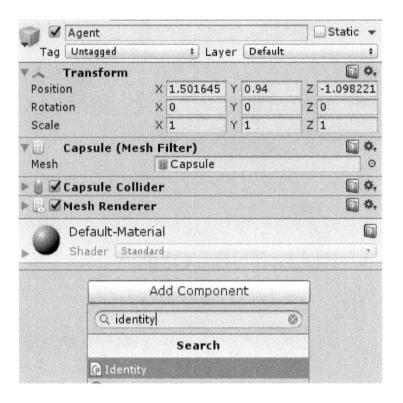

11.4 /   TUTORIAL: THE EXPLANATION

This is just a very simple way of storing basic information about a particular agent. The script comprises only variables. This should be attached to all agents and even the human player. Later, other scripts will refer to this component. For example, our *charClass* variable will be used for targeting purposes, if we elect to target a particular class of enemies.

12 / HEALTH SYSTEM

12.1 /   INTRODUCTION

The Health module manages the health-related stats for an agent, and primarily serves to track remaining health, and receive commands to either heal or cause damage. In this chapter, we will create our health system that can receive damage and call special effects on certain events such as on damage received and death.

This chapter begins with a concept guide, and some reference code. This code is not part of the Health system coding tutorial yet. The actual source code for this health system comes later in this chapter.

The Health Module, in relation to the Central Brain and External Objects

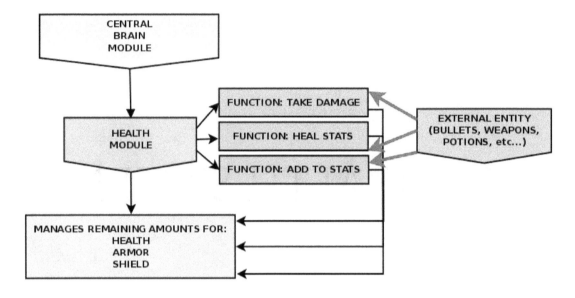

The Health module can be programmatically represented by a set of variables (Health, Armor, Shield, Regeneration Rate) and 3 main functions (TakeDamage, HealStates, and AddToStats).

Important Variables

Health: The remaining health of the agent. When this reaches 0, the agent is considered terminated.

Armor: An amount that is deducted from incoming damage, before hitting the health.

Shield: The remaining shield of the agent. In contrast to armor, shields can completely absorb incoming damage, preventing minimal damage from reaching the Health variable. When shields are depleted, it will no longer prevent damage.

Regeneration Rate: The health regeneration rate, usually defined by a static amount of health regenerated per time period. For example, if your Regeneration Rate is 5 per second, then every second of game time you would run a function that will add 5 to remaining Health.

In Unity, the Regeneration Rate can be programatically represented using InvokeRepeating:

```
float health = 100;
float regenRate = 5;

void Start () {
   // Triggers RegenerateHealth method every 1 second, beginning in 1 second
   InvokeRepeating("RegenerateHealth", 1, 1);
}

void RegenerateHealth(){
   if (health < 100){
        health = health + regenRate;
   }
}
```

12.2 /   TUTORIAL: THE SETUP

Create a new script named "Health" and attach it to our Agent object:

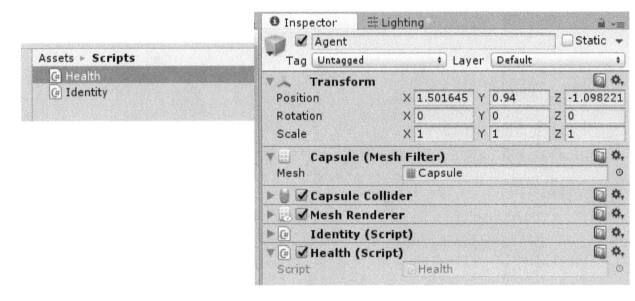

12.3 /   TUTORIAL: THE CODE

Open the script in your editor. First, we'll set up the variables we will be using. So insert the following variables into the script:

```
using UnityEngine;
using System.Collections;


public class Health : MonoBehaviour {
    public float health = 100f;
    private float maxHealth;   // do not set in editor
    public float armor = 0;
    public float healthRegenRate = 2f;
```

```
public bool godMode = false;


public string onHitFunction = "";

public string onDeathFunction = "";


// RUNTIME USE:

public bool alive = true;

public float lastDamage = 0;
```

PERFORMANCE NOTE: Go down to Update() and type in the following note:

```
// Update is called once per frame
void Update () {
     // do not put anything in here
}
```

Why? This is a developer's note to yourself to remind you to avoid using Unity's Update() function for what we're doing. If, at a later point, you decide to expand on the featureset, you're free to add what you want. The reason for this is because Update() runs constantly and doing so for potentially many agents in a scene (or hundreds for large battle scenes) can be a performance hit. It's good practice to avoid placing code into Update() as much as possible, unless your function absolutely requires real time processing. In our example here, we removed the Update() code block altogether.

First off, let's set maxHealth to health on start:

```
// Use this for initialization
void Start () {
```

```
        maxHealth = health;
    }
```

Next we create the most important function of the Health component: The damage taker. So add this new method, TakeDamage() into the script:

```
public void TakeDamage(float damageAmt){
    if (alive && !godMode){
        float finalDamageAmt;
        finalDamageAmt = damageAmt - armor;

        // deduct damage from health after armor
        if (finalDamageAmt > 0){
            health = health - finalDamageAmt;
        }

        lastDamage = finalDamageAmt;

            // check if we should be dead:
            if (health <= 0){
                alive = false;
            }
    }
}
```

TakeDamage() will be called by other scripts to deal damage to this particular agent. So calling TakeDamage(15) will deal 15 damage. If this agent has armor, then the 15 damage will first be reduced by the armor amount before being subtracted from health.

We now give the agent the ability to regenerate health. Add another method called HealthRegen():

```
void HealthRegen(){
        if (healthRegenRate > 0 && health > 0){
                if (alive && (health < maxHealth)){
                        if (health + healthRegenRate > maxHealth){
                                health = maxHealth;
                        } else {
                                health = health + healthRegenRate;
                        }
                }
        }
}
```

HealthRegen will be used as an *InvokeRepeating* to regenerate health per set amount of time.

In Unity, the default Start() method is called only once per the lifetime of a script. We could call our *HealthRegen()* method in Start() using InvokeRepeating, where it will only be called once for the rest of the scene. But what if things later became complex and something happens where the Invoke is canceled? The result will be a bug: The agent will stop regenerating health, even when it's supposed to. So instead, we will use Unity's *OnEnable()* method, which is triggered every time this script component is enabled. So add the following to the script:

```
void OnEnable(){
    InvokeRepeating("HealthRegen", 1, 1);
}
```

This tells the program to call HealthRegen() every 1 second, starting at 1 second. Obviously you can set this number to any amount you wish. If you want to regenerate health every 0.5 seconds, set it to 0.5 instead of 1.

But what if things later get complex and something happens that disables this script component? Well, in Unity, when a script is disabled (whether you uncheck it manually in the Inspector, or disable it at runtime), any InvokeRepeatings that it had running are **not** removed, meaning, they will keep running. So if you, for some reason, needed to disable or delete this Health script at runtime, the InvokeRepeating for *HealthRegen* will continue to run. Since we used *OnEnable()*, we also need to tell the program to cease regenerating health, when the script ever becomes disabled. Otherwise, the InvokeRepeating will continue to run, regenerating health every few seconds even after the script is disabled. We can do this with Unity's *OnDisable()*:

```
void OnDisable(){
   CancelInvoke("HealthRegen");
   // alternatively, we could use CancelInvoke(); where it will cancel all
}
```

Next, add a new function called CheckHealth():

```
void CheckHealth(){
      if (health <= 0){
            alive = false;
      }
}
```

When health drops to or below 0, it will set the *alive* flag to false. Other scripts can check whether an agent is alive or not by checking if its Health component's *alive* variable is false.

Like RegenHealth(), this will be used in an InvokeRepeating to check health every few miliseconds. As you realize, this means we won't be checking health in real time. And that is because we do not expect every single agent in the scene to be taking damage or getting destroyed constantly, so checking health in real time would be a waste of CPU - these CPU resources can be better spent making another part of your game better. Alternatively, we could have placed this code inside Update() or FixedUpdate() but that is usually not performance optimized.

Similar to what we did for RegenHealth(), we will initialize the InvokeRepeating in the OnEnable() method, so update OnEnable() like so:

```
void OnEnable(){
        InvokeRepeating("HealthRegen", 1, 1);
        InvokeRepeating("CheckHealth", 0.5f, 0.5f);
}
```

And again, we must tell the program to cancel these in case the script becomes disabled:

```
void OnDisable(){
   CancelInvoke("HealthRegen");
   CancelInvoke("CheckHealth");
   // alternatively, we could use CancelInvoke(); where it will cancel all
}
```

An essential feature of most games is the ability to heal a character. Let's create a new function called Heal():

```
public void Heal(float healAmt){
        health += healAmt;
        if (health > maxHealth){
                health = maxHealth;
        }
}
```

Other scripts can heal this agent by calling the *Heal()* method of the Health component on this agent. *Example: agentObject.GetComponent<Health>().Heal(15) to heal 15 points.*

At a certain time, you may need the ability to revive a dead agent. We'll give the agent a simple and quick revive ability with the following new public method, Revive():

```
public void Revive(){
        health = maxHealth;
        alive = true;
}
```

And finally, for convenience purposes, let's give our other scripts a quick way to determine the agent's remaining percentage of health. This can be useful, especially when creating advanced agent behavior, such as fleeing when health is below a certain percentage, or displaying remaining health percent onto UI such as a HUD.

Add a new public method called GetHealthPercentage():

```
public float GetHealthPercentage(){
        float perc;

        perc = (health / maxHealth) * 100f;

        return Mathf.Round(perc);
}
```

Example use:

```
float healthPerc = agentObject.GetComponent<Health>().GetHealthPercentage();

// the above will return a number between 0 and 100.
```

That's it for this Health module. This can certainly be expanded upon but for the sake of this tutorial, we will leave it has is.

Here is the entire code:

12.4 / ENTIRE CODE: HEALTH.CS

```csharp
using UnityEngine;
using System.Collections;

public class Health : MonoBehaviour {

    public float health = 100f;
    private float maxHealth;   // do not set in editor
    public float armor = 0;
    public float healthRegenRate = 2f;
    public bool godMode = false; // make agent invincible, take no damage
    public string onHitFunction = "";
    public string onDeathFunction = "";


    // RUNTIME USE:
    public bool alive = true;
    public float lastDamage = 0;


    // Use this for initialization
    void Start () {
        maxHealth = health;
    }


    void OnEnable(){
        InvokeRepeating("HealthRegen", 1, 1);
        InvokeRepeating("CheckHealth", 0.5f, 0.5f);
    }


    void OnDisable(){
        CancelInvoke();
```

```
        }

    public void TakeDamage(float damageAmt){
            if (alive && !godMode){
                    float finalDamageAmt;
                    finalDamageAmt = damageAmt - armor;

                    // deduct damage from health after armor
                    if (finalDamageAmt > 0){
                            health = health - finalDamageAmt;
                    }

                    lastDamage = finalDamageAmt;

                    // check if we should be dead:
                    if (health <= 0){
                            alive = false;
                    }

                    // call any external script functions on hit:
                    if (onHitFunction != ""){
                            gameObject.SendMessage(onHitFunction);
                    }
            }
    }
    void HealthRegen(){
            if (healthRegenRate > 0 && health > 0){
                    if (alive && (health < maxHealth)){
                            if (health + healthRegenRate > maxHealth){
                                    health = maxHealth;
                            } else {
                                    health = health + healthRegenRate;
                            }
```

```
            }
        }
}
void CheckHealth(){
        if (health <= 0){
                alive = false;

                // call any external script functions on hit:
                if (onHitFunction != ""){
                        gameObject.SendMessage(onDeathFunction);
                }
        }
}


public void Heal(float healAmt){
        health += healAmt;
        if (health > maxHealth){
                health = maxHealth;
        }
}


public void Revive(){
        health = maxHealth;
        alive = true;
}


public float GetHealthPercentage(){
        float perc;

        perc = (health / maxHealth) * 100f;

        return Mathf.Round(perc);
}
```

```
}
```

End Code for Health.cs

12.5 /   TUTORIAL: THE EXPLANATION

We created a separate script, Health.cs as part of our modular A.I. system to manage all health-related parameters and functions. Most of this Health component should be pretty self-explanatory: The TakeDamage() method is called by other scripts to deal damage and subtract from the *health* variable, after armor is taken into account. The agent can auto-regenerate health using the RegenHealth() with InvokeRepeating. And convenient public methods are provided for other scripts to access, such as GetHealthPercentage().

You may be wondering what the uses are for the 2 strings: onHitFunction and onDeathFunction, as well as the following code inside the TakeDamage() method:

```
if (onHitFunction != ""){
        gameObject.SendMessage(onHitFunction);
}
```

What this does is it automatically calls a function name you choose each time the agent takes damage. It uses Unity's SendMessage implementation to allow messages to be sent between scripts. For example, if you want the agent to play a specific animation using *another* attached script when it's hit by a bullet, we can use SendMessage to do it. Let's say we have another script attached that has the function, PlayHitAnimation(), which plays the animation we want. In this Health component, we set the variable *onHitFunction* to be "PlayHitAnimation" (without any parentheses or quotes). Now, whenever the agent takes damage, this Health module will trigger all functions named "PlayHitAnimation" that are attached to the agent. You do not need to specify a script name – as long as a script on the agent has that method name, that method will be triggered. As you'll see later, we will use this to play onhit and death effects for the agent.

12.6 /   TUTORIAL: TEST THE CODE

Let's quickly test that our Health script is working by using Unity's Destroy() method.
Update the CheckHealth() method with the following code:

```
void CheckHealth(){
      if (health <= 0){
            alive = false;


            Destroy(gameObject); // remove this agent from scene


            // call any external script functions on hit:
            if (onHitFunction != ""){
                  gameObject.SendMessage(onDeathFunction);
            }
      }
}
```

What this line does is it will remove the agent from the scene.

So play the scene in the editor. Do not "Maximize on Play". Then, while the scene is
playing, click on the agent and set its *Health* to 0 in the editor:

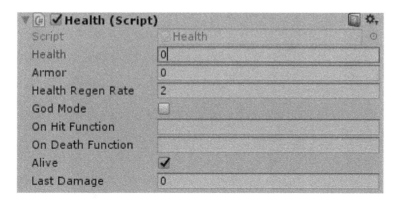

If your code is set up correctly, the agent should automatically be deleted from the scene.

13 / PERCEPTION

As we discussed earlier, an agent is defined by its ability to perceive and act. As part of our modular AI system, we will create a separate script that gathers data about the agent's nearby environment, specifically enemy and ally objects. This module only gathers data and does not make any behavior decisions or actions. But before we get to the code, let's go over some concepts first.

13.1 /   THE ILLUSION OF LIMITED PERCEPTION

Let's not fool ourselves - the perception implementations in most game A.I. mainly deals with creating the **illusion** that the A.I. has limited senses, similar to a human or animal. In reality, your computer program, and therefore your A.I., always knows where the player is, where he is hiding, and the direction of his travel. The A.I. can simply look this up by checking the 2D or 3D coordinates of the player's position. But an agent that always knows the player's information wouldn't make for a fun or realistic game. **Therefore, we simulate limited perception by actually making the A.I. *less* intelligent.** This differs significantly from the perception problems that most academic A.I. scientists are trying to solve, such as the ability for a robot on an actual battlefield to perceive nearby enemies or discern terrorists from innocent civilians. A battlefield robot may still receive GPS positions of a nearby enemy from an overhead drone, but if a person suddenly popped out from behind it, would it really know whether that's a terrorist or civilian? In the world of gaming A.I., we are lucky to never have such a problem! If an agent inside a game were to have trouble discerning friend from foe, that is only because we specifically programmed it to act foolish and ignore information that is always available to it. If you keep this in mind, you can use this to your advantage to create a wide variety of A.I., behavior styles, and enemy difficulties. Players love variation and will love your game for it. Later in this chapter we will be doing exactly this: Creating the illusion of limited perception.

13.2 /   ELEMENTS OF PERCEPTION

The Sensory and Perception Module, also called our Awareness module, gives the AI:

- Vision

- Environmental awareness

- Friend or foe identification

- Target tracking (what is the target's position?)

- Line of sight (can target be seen or is it behind an obstacle?)

- Angle of vision

- Object identification (weapon pickups, health pickups, cover spots, etc...)

- Weapon & Attack range calculations

It contains a set of variables that describe the agent's vision capabilities and faction tag recognition. Specifically, the Awareness module contains the following variables:

Sight Range: The maximum distance from which the agent can detect objects. This can usually represented by a straight line from the agent's eye position, but also by a radial zone around the agent, especially if the agent is a turret or tank unit.

Angle of Vision: The maximum angle by which an agent can detect an object. An example usage is when a target is inside an agent's Sight Range, but not directly in front of the agent. In fact, the target is a little off to the side of the agent, about 75 degrees east. If this scenario was in an online multiplayer game, a human player would probably begin shooting, spraying bullets in a wide arc, even if his target isn't directly in front of his cross-hairs. The same concept applies here to the A.I. agent. In an attempt to make the agents' behavior more similar to that of a human's, we add a bit of variation and chaos to their aiming abilities. Here, the Angle of Vision factor helps us to construct that.

Hostile Faction Tags: A list of faction IDs the agent will identify as enemy targets. This list is programatically represented as an array object. For example, in Unity, these can simply be the standard game object tags.

Friendly Faction Tags: Like the hostile faction tags, the Friendly Tags are a list of faction IDs the agent will identify as friendly agents. An example use case is in calculating the ratio of enemies to allies around the agent. If the ratio is too high, the agent should call in back up.

Object Identification: Like the faction tags, object identification also uses a list of tags to identify certain objects. For example, health potions can be tagged as "Health Items" and weapon pickups can be tagged as "Weapon." As the agent travels around the game world, it will constantly scan its nearby area for objects with these tags.

13.3 / LINE OF SIGHT

Line of Sight in an important concept in gaming and is used to determine whether an agent can see an object. This differs from Sight Range in that sight range simply tells an agent how *far* it can see, while Line of Sight restricts an agent's sight to what it can *actually* see. Specifically, the objects that the agent can actually see are objects that are not blocked by obstacles between them and the agent. In almost all game engines, sight can be simulated by attempting to draw a line from the agent to the object in question. We call this line a "raycast". While you do not need to understand the underlying math behind raycasts, you must be familiar with their purposes and uses. At the most basic level, a raycast is simply a line drawn from one point in either 2D (x, y) or 3D (x, y, z) space to another point in the game world. How is this used to simulate agent sight? Think like this: If a line can be drawn from the agent's position to a target object's position, without overlapping any other objects along the way, then we can conclude that the object is in the agent's line of sight. However, if we fail to draw a direct line from the agent to its target, such as when our line touches an obstacle like a wall, before it reaches the target object, then we can assume that the target not within line of sight.

For example, assume there is an agent with a Sight Range of 50 units standing in front of a wall. An enemy agent is on the other side of the wall and the distance between them is 30, which is inside the agent's Sight Range. To test whether the enemy is within line of sight, we draw a line (raycast) from the agent to the enemy. In this case, the line will hit the wall obstacle before it reaches the enemy. As a result, our program then determines that the enemy is not within line of sight, despite it being inside the agent's sight range.

Line of Sight: Determines which objects within agent's Sight Range (blue zone) can be detected (see diagram on next page).

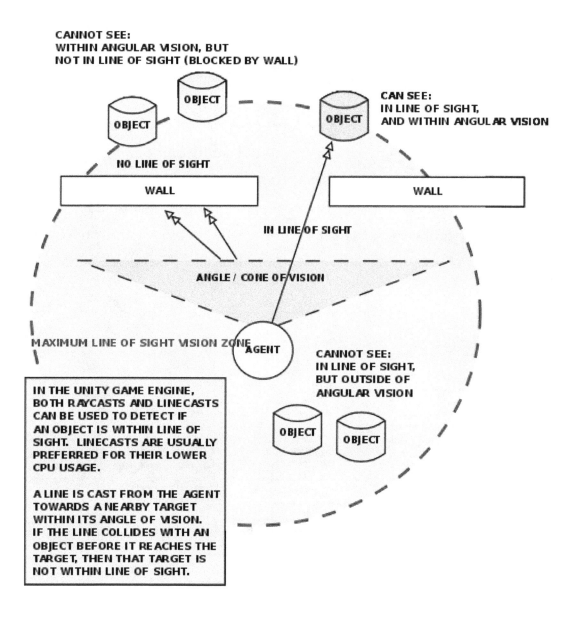

CANNOT SEE:
WITHIN ANGULAR VISION, BUT
NOT IN LINE OF SIGHT (BLOCKED BY WALL)

OBJECT

OBJECT

CAN SEE:
IN LINE OF SIGHT,
AND WITHIN ANGULAR VISION

OBJECT

NO LINE OF SIGHT

WALL

WALL

IN LINE OF SIGHT

ANGLE / CONE OF VISION

MAXIMUM LINE OF SIGHT VISION ZONE

AGENT

CANNOT SEE:
IN LINE OF SIGHT,
BUT OUTSIDE OF
ANGULAR VISION

OBJECT   OBJECT

IN THE UNITY GAME ENGINE,
BOTH RAYCASTS AND LINECASTS
CAN BE USED TO DETECT IF
AN OBJECT IS WITHIN LINE OF
SIGHT. LINECASTS ARE USUALLY
PREFERRED FOR THEIR LOWER
CPU USAGE.

A LINE IS CAST FROM THE AGENT
TOWARDS A NEARBY TARGET
WITHIN ITS ANGLE OF VISION.
IF THE LINE COLLIDES WITH AN
OBJECT BEFORE IT REACHES THE
TARGET, THEN THAT TARGET IS
NOT WITHIN LINE OF SIGHT.

In this diagram, the agent wants to determine whether any of the Objects (gray) are within its line of sight, so that it can take action against the objects. The agent will loop through each nearby object and fire a raycast towards them. The only object within the agent's line of sight is the green one, which is inside the Agent's sight range, within its angle of vision, and not blocked by an obstacle or wall.

13.4 / EXAMPLE DECISION TREE: ACTING ON PERCEPTION

The Awareness module's primary function is to gather environment data. Thus, it must be used in conjunction with the Combat, Health, and other modules. Here is an example of a simple decision tree that is triggered when the Awareness module detects an object. Remember, this Awareness module does not actually perform any actions - it simply gathers environment data. The following chart is an example of what another script can do after receiving data from the Awareness module:

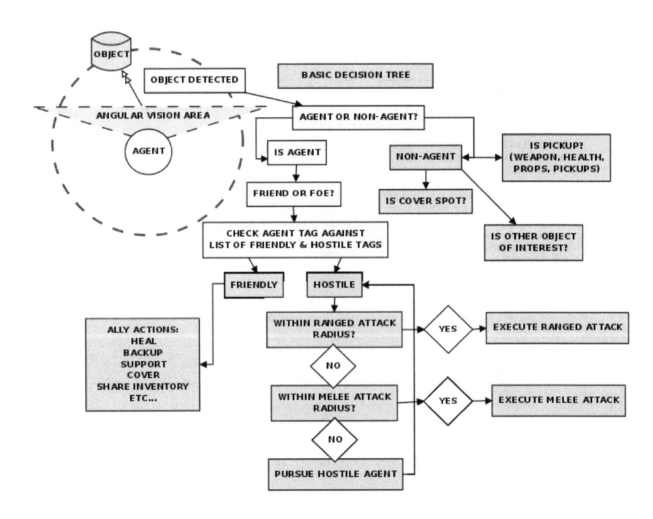

The decision tree can branch off to trigger further actions by the agent, such as healing an ally (if the object is identified as an ally), picking up a weapon (if the object is recognized as a weapon pick up), or executing an attack (if the object is identified as an enemy). Additionally, if the Awareness module determines that the object is hostile, but outside of its attack range, the decision tree can branch off to trigger a Chase event, where the agent pursues the target until it's close enough to be attacked.

Let's put this into practice by coding our Awareness component.

13.5 /   TUTORIAL: THE SETUP

Like before, create a new script and name it Awareness.cs. Attach this new Awareness component to the agent object. So our agent's component list should now look like this:

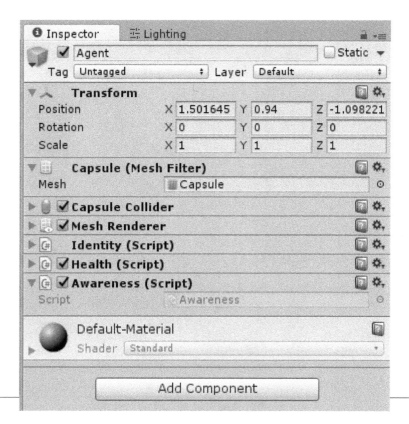

Right-click the agent object and click "Create Empty" to create a new blank gameobject as a child. Name this new object, "Scan position":

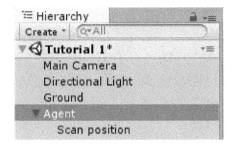

This represents the position to scan the environment, which we will use later in our code. For humanoid models, this is usually placed at the eye level, but for our purposes here, drag this new object towards to top of the agent:

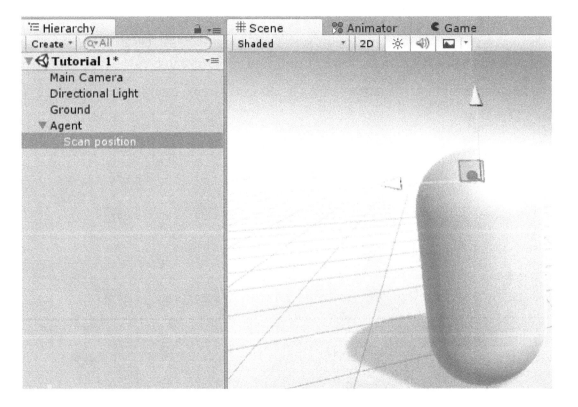

13.6 / TUTORIAL: THE CODE

Open up the new Awareness.cs script you just added and let's first insert the variables we need. Don't worry if you don't understand why some variables exist, we will explain all of them in this chapter.

Important: We'll be using C#'s handy List object to store our nearby enemies and allies. Therefore, we will need to add *using System.Collections.Generic* to the top of the script, where *using UnityEngine;* is.

```csharp
using System.Collections.Generic;
using UnityEngine;
using System.Collections;

public class Awareness : MonoBehaviour {
    [Header("Sight Position")]
    public Transform scannerPosition;


    [Header("Set hostile factions:")]
    public string[] enemyFactions;


    [Header("Set friendly factions: (exclude AI own tag)")]
    public string[] friendlyFactions;


    [Header("How far can the AI see?")]
    [Range(0, 999)]
    public float sightRange = 75f;


    [Header("Field of View Angle")]
    [Range(0, 360)]
    public float angleOfSight = 300f;
```

```
[Header("RUNTIME USE")]
public List<GameObject> enemyList = new List<GameObject>();
public List<GameObject> allyList = new List<GameObject>();
```

Like our Health component, delete the Update() method for performance reasons since we won't be using it. **Even if the Update() method is empty, it will still use CPU and we want to squeeze out every little bit of performance we can.** The Start() method is also empty, but we'll leave it there in case you need to use it later.

As you might've predicted, since we removed Update(), we'll be using InvokeRepeating to continuously capture nearby data. And, like what we did in the previous Health chapter, we'll be using Unity's OnEnable() and OnDisable() to manage the InvokeRepeatings, instead of Start().

Let's add in our OnEnable() and OnDisable() code now. The following will trigger errors if you run it now because the method UpdatePlayerLists() doesn't exist yet. Ignore the error and continue on with this tutorial:

```
void OnEnable(){
        InvokeRepeating("UpdatePlayerLists", 1, 1);
}

void OnDisable(){
        CancelInvoke();
}
```

How can we check whether our agent can see a target? We will use Unity's *Physics.OverlapSphere()* method to create an invisible sphere at runtime at the agent's position, with a radial size of the sight range variable we created earlier. We will then retrieve every single object that touches this invisible sphere. We will loop through each touched object and check whether the object is within the agent's sight range, angle of sight, and line of sight. Finally, if we determine that this object fulfills all 3 conditions (sight range, angle, line of sight), we will check this object's tag against our *enemyFactions* and *friendlyFactions* lists. Our next step, therefore, is to build the functions that will determine if an object is within sight range, sight angle, line of sight, and whether it's an enemy or friend. These functions will be public functions so that if needed, other scripts can access them for convenience.

The function for checking if an object is within sight angle:

```
public bool IsObjectWithinSightAngle(Transform t){
      Vector3 direction = t.position - scannerPosition.position;
      float objectAngle = Vector3.Angle (direction,
                                          scannerPosition.forward);
      return (objectAngle <= angleOfSight);
}
```

The function for checking if an object is within line of sight, meaning, there are no obstacles in the way between the agent and the object:

```
public bool IsObjectWithinLOS(Transform t){
      RaycastHit losHit;

      if (Physics.Linecast(scannerPosition.position, t.position, out
                                                       losHit)){
            return (losHit.transform == t);
      }
      return false;
}
```

The function to check if a string is an enemy faction:

```
public bool IsEnemyFaction(string objFac){
        bool isEnemy = false;
        foreach(string enemyFaction in enemyFactions){
                if (enemyFaction == objFac){
                        isEnemy = true;
                }
        }


        return isEnemy;
}
```

The function to check if a string is a friendly faction:

```
public bool IsAllyFaction(string objFac){
        bool isAlly = false;
        foreach(string friendlyFaction in friendlyFactions){
                if (friendlyFaction == objFac){
                        isAlly = true;
                }
        }


        return isAlly;
}
```

To check if an object is within sight range, we will not use a separate function, but rather we let the sight range be automatically taken into consideration when casting an invisible sphere to check for nearby object collisions. This check will be done in the next and final function.

Now we put these functions together and update our nearby enemies and friends lists.

Create a new method called UpdatePlayerLists() with the following code:

13.7 /   AWARENESS.CS

```
public void UpdatePlayerLists(){
      enemyList.Clear();
      allyList.Clear();


      Collider[] objectsWithinSight = new Collider[10];


      objectsWithinSight = Physics.OverlapSphere (scannerPosition.position,
sightRange);
      GameObject tempTarget;      // temp holds the object we're scanning


      for (int i=0; i< objectsWithinSight.Length; i++) {
          // grab this temporary object so we can check it:
          tempTarget = objectsWithinSight[i].transform.gameObject;


          // first do a check - this scanned object
          // is not the agent itself:
          if (tempTarget != gameObject){


          // check if hit obj is enemy?
          if (IsEnemyFaction(tempTarget.tag)){
          if (IsObjectWithinSightAngle(tempTarget.transform)){
          // enemy within sight angle...now check if within LOS:
          if (IsObjectWithinLOS(tempTarget.transform)){
          // check if temp target alive:
          if (tempTarget.GetComponent<Health>() != null){
                  if (tempTarget.GetComponent<Health>().enabled == false ||
                      tempTarget.GetComponent<Health>().alive != false){
                      // this is a viable enemy, so add him to our list:
```

```
                        enemyList.Add(tempTarget);
            }
        } else {
            // this is a viable enemy, so add him to our list:
            enemyList.Add(tempTarget);
        }
        }
        }
        }


        // is obj ally?
        else if (IsAllyFaction(tempTarget.tag)){
            // object is ally...we're not going to check LOS or angle
            // because we should know where each ally pos is anyways
            allyList.Add(tempTarget);
        }
    }
    }
}
```

End Code for Awareness.cs

That's it for the Awareness / Perception module. This last method we just created, UpdatePlayerLists(), should be called using an InvokeRepeating at a set interval. We've already done this earlier in the chapter, when we placed InvokeRepeating() under the OnEnable() method.

13.8 /   TUTORIAL: THE EXPLANATION

In the final function, we used Unity's *Physics.OverlapSphere()* method to first cast an invisible sphere from the agent's position and extending out at a radial distance of our *sightRange* variable. We gathered every object (with Collider) that was hit by this sphere, looped through each, and ran a test to see whether that object was within our agent's sight range, sight angle, and line of sight.

The sight range test was automatically taken care of when we cast the invisible sphere at the size of our sight range.

The sight angle test was done by first getting the Vector direction from our agent to the object and then checking the angle from the agent's forward vector to the direction vector. Unity's built-in Vector3.Angle() method was very convenient in this case.

The line of sight test was done by using Unity's *Physics.Linecast()* method to draw an invisible line from the agent to the object. If the invisible line is successfully drawn, then the object is considered to be within line of sight. But if the line does not reach the object, meaning, it hits another object while being drawn, then the object is not within line of sight. Note: We specifically chose *Physics.Linecast()* over the more popular *Physics.Raycast()* for performance reasons. In our experience, *Physics.Linecast()* is very fast and light on performance – the perfect way to simulate line of sight. You could have alternatively used *Physics.Raycast()* instead of *Linecast()* and would have gotten the same result.

Finally, we checked whether this object is an enemy or friend by running it through our handy functions, *IsEnemyFaction()* and *IsAllyFaction()*, which loops through our List of specified enemy and friendly tags. The check is done simply by checking the Tag of the object with gameObject.tag.

13.9 / TUTORIAL: TEST THE CODE

Even though the rest of our agent hasn't been coded yet, we can still test and confirm that our Awareness module is working by checking if the Awareness module correctly finds nearby enemy objects.

1) In your scene, select the Agent and go to the Awareness component we just created. Find the *Enemy Factions* slot and create a new slot. Insert "Team2" into that slot like so:

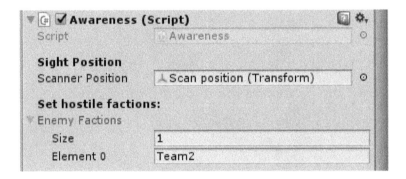

2) Insert a cube into the scene and place it near the agent. Rename the cube as "Enemy":

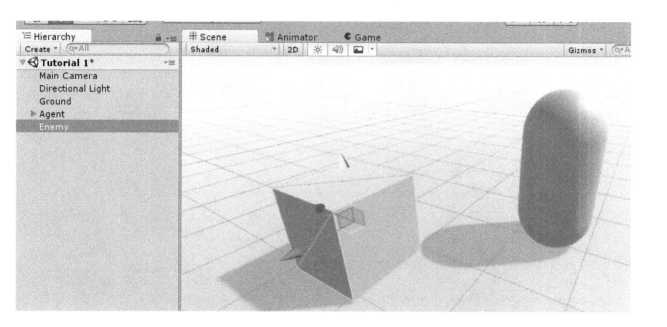

3) Add 2 tags to your project: Team1, Team2:

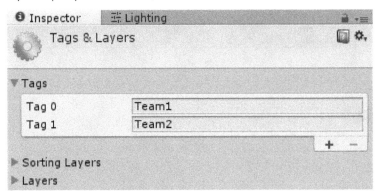

4) Now select and tag your cube as Team2:

5) Duplicate this cube twice, making 3 enemy objects and place each nearby the agent.

Your scene should look something like this:

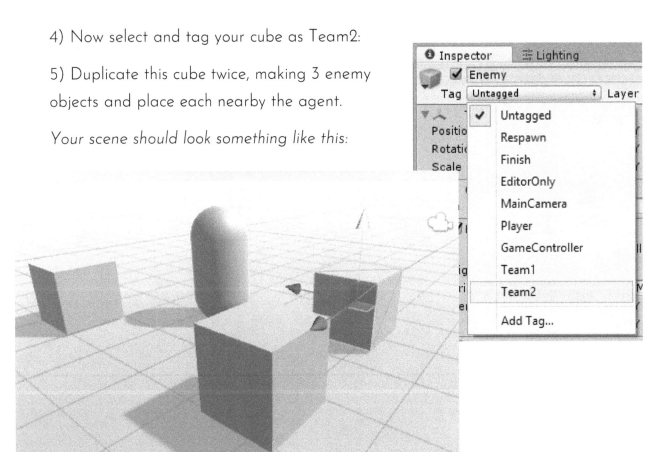

6) For the final step, we will run the scene and test if our Awareness module is
working.

So select the Agent object again and play the scene.

If you had entered the code correctly, then a few seconds after the scene plays, 3
enemies should show up in the *Enemy List* of the Agent's Awareness Module, like this:

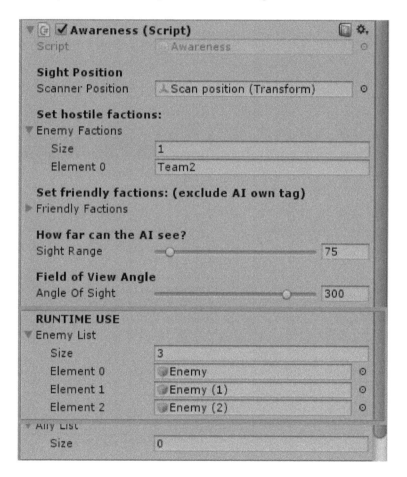

When you see this, that means the Awareness module we just coded successfully
detected the 3 nearby enemies. You can optionally test the sight range by playing the
scene, switching back to Scene View at runtime, and dragging a cube far away from
the agent, outside of its sight range. This *Enemy List* should then drop to 2 enemies

instead of 3.

14 / COMBAT SYSTEM

14.1 / INTRODUCTION

The Combat module gives the A.I. attack capabilities, specifically, the ability to operate a weapon. It includes the functionality to launch projectiles, deal damage, play weapon audio, generate special effects, and play attack animations. The combat module dynamically loads active weapons and processes their data. For example, assume an agent has both a shotgun and rocket launcher in its inventory. On making the shotgun active, the Combat Module will fire shotgun projectile types that deal 50 damage, play a shotgun sound, generate a shotgun muzzle flash, and play an animation of the agent firing the weapon. Later, the agent switches to the rocket launcher. Now, the Combat module will load similar data from the rocket launcher, such as what projectile to fire (rockets), damage type (100 damage), audio (blast sounds), and more.

A weapon type consists of a raw weapon model or graphic, and a list of weapon statistics, such as weapon name, projectile type, fire rate, starting ammo, starting clips, damage, etc. These statistics are then loaded into the Combat module when the agent switches to the weapon.

14.2 / RANGED ATTACKS

A projectile, utilized by ranged weapons, consists of a raw bullet or rocket model or graphic and a list of bullet statistics, such as bullet name and damage, a small collision detection area, special effects to spawn on hit, and the capability to communicate with an agent's health module in order to deal damage. A projectile's properties are loaded into the Combat module.

A crucial element of a ranged weapon system is the capability to send a projectile across the game scene. Depending on your game engine, the simplest method is to use the basic forward movement function - the same function that powers the agent in the movement module, using the Translate() method:

```
public GameObject bulletObject; // this holds the bullet type to be fired
float bulletSpeed = 1000;
void FixedUpdate(){
   // fire bullet forward using translate (less CPU usage):
   myTransform.Translate(0,0, (Time.deltaTime * bulletSpeed));
}
```

A more realistic method is to power projectile flight with a game engine's built-in physics kit. Most 2D and 3D game engines have physics simulation capabilities built-in, particularly Unity, Unreal, and CryEngine. For HTML5 games, an open source physics kit, Box 2D, can power 2D games and Three can powered 3D games. In Unity, shooting a projectile using physics is quite simple and involves a GameObject with an attached Rigidbody.

```
public GameObject bulletObject; // this holds the bullet type to be fired
float bulletSpeed = 1000;
Rigidbody bulletRigidBody = BulletObject.GetComponent<Rigidbody>();
// shoot the bullet:
bulletRigidBody.AddForce(bulletObject.transform.forward * bulletSpeed);
```

Performance Note: *Physics-driven Rigidbody bullets are not recommended if your scene involves hundreds of bullets.*

14.3 / ATTACK RANGE

The Awareness module is also used to determine whether a target is within the attack range. Attack Range is similar to Sight Range. For an target to be considered within attack range, it must be both positioned within Sight Range and the Attack Range.

Here, Target A is inside sight range, but cannot be seen. Target B is inside sight range, but outside attack range and cannot be attacked.

(see diagram on next page)

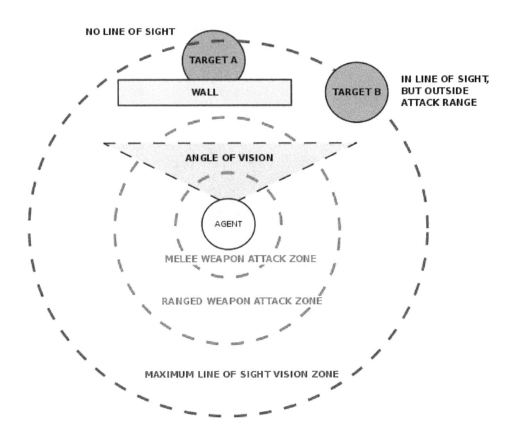

The Target is inside both Sight and Attack range, which will trigger the Combat module on the agent.

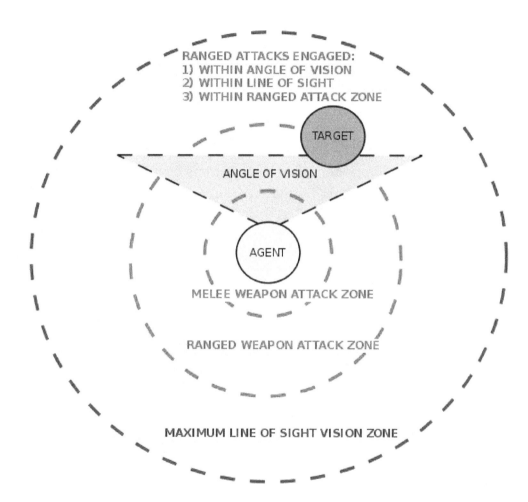

14.4 /   SIMULATING SHOT *INACCURACY*

You might have expected that, as A.I. developers, we would seek to make the A.I. as intelligent and skilled as possible. That would have been true for usual research ventures in A.I., but not for our game dev case. In our case, we actually want to give our agents the ability to be *inaccurate* to make them more human like! We want our agents to make human-like mistakes. We want to give our human players a chance to exploit an agent's weakness, either in shot accuracy or some other handicap. As we mentioned before, a virtual opponent that always aims and hits its target with 100% accuracy can be boring, predictable, and frustrating to play against. And, given the demands of today's gamers, it's in the developer's best interest to create agents that boast a variety of skills, firepower, and stats. One of the simplest ways to accomplish that is to add randomness to an agent's weapon handling. When an agent acquires a target, a small random variable should be added to the target's position. This random variable will force the agent to aim a small distance away from the target, ensuring that the agent will sometimes miss the shot. Decreasing that random variable will create agents with higher shot accuracy and increasing it will decrease shot accuracy. This simple implementation adds a great deal of realism to a combat scenario.

In Unity, shot accuracy can be simulated in the following manner:

```
public Transform target;
public float inaccuracy = 2; // random amount to be added/subtracted


Vector3 targetPosition = target.position; // get the Vector3 position


// add randomness to the target position, using inaccuracy
// set the new coordinates
float xPos = targetPosition.x + Random.Range(-inaccuracy, inaccuracy);
```

```
float yPos = targetPosition.y + Random.Range(-inaccuracy, inaccuracy);

float zPos = targetPosition.z + Random.Range(-inaccuracy, inaccuracy);


// define the actual position the agent should aim at

Vector3 newTargetPosition = new Vector3 (xPos, yPos, zPos);


// the rest of your code goes here…

// you would add a rotation function that rotates the agent's aiming towards

// newTargetPosition instead of targetPosition
```

14.5 / MELEE ATTACKS

Melee weapons, such as swords, fists, axes, and even moving cars, send damage to an object when its collision boundaries overlap with that object. Such weapons are made up of a raw 3D model or graphic, a defined collision area (usually the edges of the model itself), special effects to spawn on hit, and the capability to communicate with the victim agent's health module to deal damage.

Dealing damage with a melee weapon is fairly straightforward to implement. Most popular game engines give you tools to define a collision boundary around a model or graphic. In Unity, this boundary is called a "collider", and can be any collider such as a box collider, sphere collider, or mesh collider. This collider is attached to a weapon model in order to trigger damage functions. The following diagram shows a sword weapon setup with a simple rectangular collider (box collider in Unity). Notice that the collider does not overlap the bottom of the sword, which is where the agent will have his hands. This is to prevent the weapon from sending damage to the agent himself or causing unnecessary collision events.

(see next page for diagram)

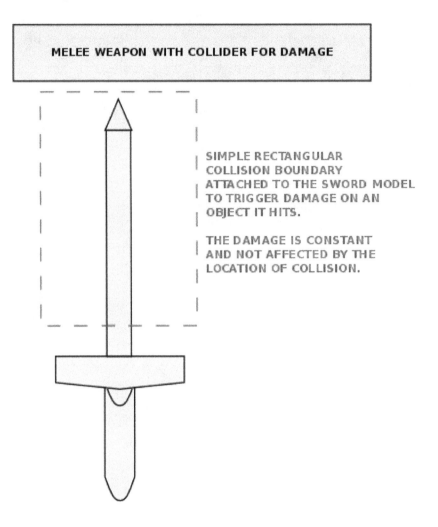

MELEE WEAPON WITH COLLIDER FOR DAMAGE

SIMPLE RECTANGULAR COLLISION BOUNDARY ATTACHED TO THE SWORD MODEL TO TRIGGER DAMAGE ON AN OBJECT IT HITS.

THE DAMAGE IS CONSTANT AND NOT AFFECTED BY THE LOCATION OF COLLISION.

This simple implementation of a collider-based melee damage system has the sword dealing constant damage throughout the collider, unaffected by the location of the actual collision. In the next diagram, we show a multi-collider design that allows for varying amounts of damage, depending on where the weapon hits.

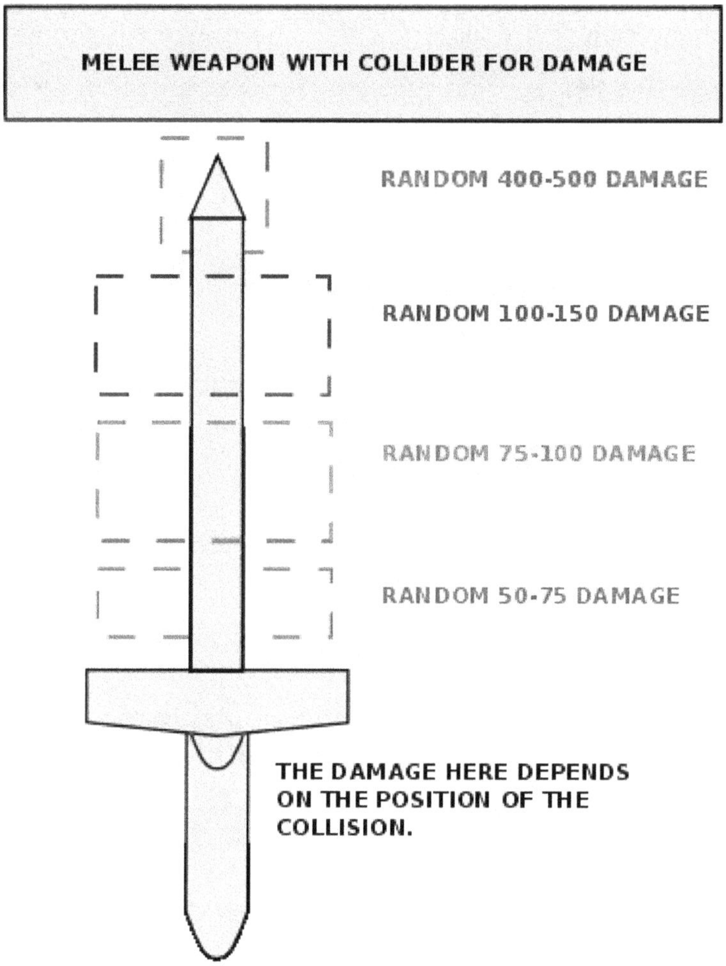

MELEE WEAPON WITH COLLIDER FOR DAMAGE

RANDOM 400-500 DAMAGE

RANDOM 100-150 DAMAGE

RANDOM 75-100 DAMAGE

RANDOM 50-75 DAMAGE

THE DAMAGE HERE DEPENDS ON THE POSITION OF THE COLLISION.

The melee weapon shown here employs multiple damage colliders. The tip of the sword, typically used for thrusting, is fit with a small collider to cause critical damage. The rest of the colliders all deal varying amounts of damage. To implement this system, simply use an if-then condition to check which collider was hit and deal the appropriate damage. In Unity, multiple colliders can be attached to an object, but it may be difficult to determine which exact one was involved in a collision. The solution in Unity is to attach empty GameObjects as child objects of the weapon model. Each empty GameObject is attached with its own trigger collider. You can then move each collider to the position of your choosing. To deal damage, you can attach a script to each attached GameObject that attempts to call the damage function (Health module) of the object it colliders with. The melee system we will be implementing will use the simpler single-collider implementation instead of multiple colliders.

14.6 /   TUTORIAL: THE SETUP

Let's get started creating our combat system that supports both melee and ranged attacks. Before we code, we first have to set up our bullet prefab and the on-hit particles which will later be loaded into our scripts.

CREATING THE BULLET

1) In your scene, insert a Sphere object from the GameObject menu. Drag the Sphere into view and above ground.

2) Set the Scale of the Sphere to (0.2, 0.2, 0.2):

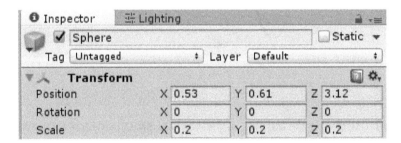

3) Set the Sphere Collider to *Is Trigger*:

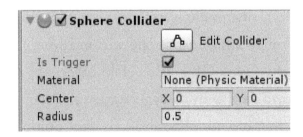

Later in the code, we will use this collider trigger to detect whether the bullet hit an object and whether that object is an actor we can send damage to.

4) Rename the Sphere to "Bullet".

5) Add a Rigidbody component to the bullet. Uncheck *Use Gravity*. Add this Rigidbody even if you won't be using physics-driven bullet motion. That's because Unity's OnTriggerEnter() method that we will be using later requires either the bullet or the object it hits to have a Rigidbody in order to register the collision. By adding the Rigidbody to the bullet itself, we remove the requirement for our other objects to need one as well, such as walls and other obstacles. If you will be using physics-driven bullet motion, then this Rigidbody component is required anyways.

6) Finally, let's give the bullet a tracer-like trail so we can better identify the bullets during gameplay. Attach a Trail Renderer to the Bullet object and make the settings like so:

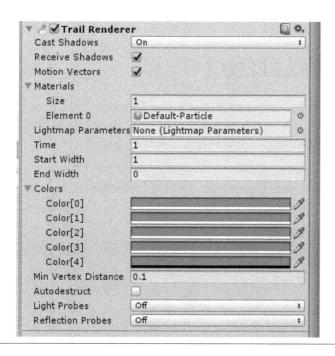

Remember to set the Materials to "Default-Particle" (included with Unity) or the trail will come out pink (missing material).

We're done setting up the bullet object. Before we begin coding, we need to create a simple on-hit effect. On-hit effects are spawned when the bullet hits any object. These can be anything such as sparks or blood particle effects.

CREATE ON-HIT PARTICLE EFFECT

1) Add a Particle System to the scene using the GameObject menu:

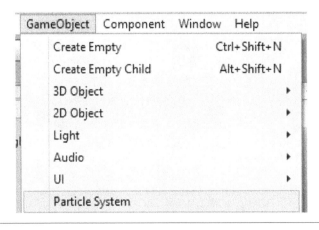

2) Drag the new Particle System around the scene until you can see it. The default effect is a constant burst of particles.

3) Rename the Particle System to "On Hit Sparks".

4) On the Particle System component, set the *Start Size* to 0.5. Set *Start Color* to orange. Set *Looping* to false by unchecking it. Set the *Duration* to 1. This tells the particle to send an orange burst one time for 1 second only.

5) Create a new folder in /Assets/ called "Prefabs"

6) For the final step, drag the On Hit Sparks object into the new Prefabs folder to make it a prefab. Later, we will load this effect into our bullet object to be spawned on collision.

From now on, whenever this book mentions making an object into a prefab, this is how it's done – by dragging the object from the scene into the "Prefabs" folder to be re-used later.

Turn an object into a prefab to be re-used by future scripts:

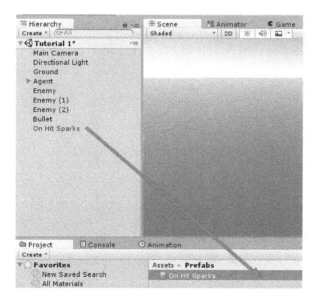

Delete the On Hit Sparks object from the scene, but do not delete the prefab from the Prefabs folder.

We're done setting up our objects. Get ready to code.

14.7 /   TUTORIAL: THE CODE

Let's finish creating our bullet by adding the necessary code. Create a new script in the /Scripts/ folder, name it "Projectile.cs" and attach the script to the Bullet object in the scene.

This projectile script comprises 3 main elements: A mechanism to propel the bullet forwards using a simple performance-focused implementation, a mechanism to propel the bullet using Rigidbody physics, and the ability to deal damage to another agent or player when it collides with them. This script will give you the option to switch between simple or physics-driven bullet movement to maximize your flexibility.

We'll start with the motor mechanism that propels the bullet forward, so update the Projectile.cs script like so:

```
using UnityEngine;
using System.Collections;


public class Projectile : MonoBehaviour {

    public float bulletForce = 100f;
    public bool useRigidbodyForce = false;
    public float damage = 15f;
```

```csharp
public float secondsToSelfDestruct = 5f;

public GameObject onHitEffect;

private Transform myTransform;


void Start(){

    // cache our transform for faster performance:

    myTransform = transform;

}


void OnEnable(){

    // Rigidbody Physics mode:

    if (useRigidbodyForce && GetComponent<Rigidbody>() != null){

        Rigidbody r = GetComponent<Rigidbody>();

        Vector3 forwardDir =
            myTransform.TransformDirection(Vector3.forward);


        // reset previous physics:

        r.velocity = Vector3.zero;

        r.AddForce(forwardDir * bulletForce);

    }


    Invoke("DestroyBullet", secondsToSelfDestruct);

}


void FixedUpdate(){

    // Simple movement mode:

    if (!useRigidbodyForce){

        myTransform.Translate(0,0, (Time.deltaTime * bulletForce));

    }

}


void DestroyBullet(){

    Destroy(gameObject);
```

```
    }
}
```

Here, the Physics-driven bullet movement is placed inside OnEnable(). That's because the physics-force is only called once, when this bullet is spawned. Once you add Rigidbody force to the bullet, Unity's physics engine will automatically push the bullet forward every frame. Any objects it collides with may be pushed back, depending on the amount of force, Rigidbody drag, and sizes of objects.

The simpler, non-physics movement mode is placed inside FixedUpdate() because we want to manually propel the bullet forward every frame. This ignores physics forces which will increase game performance significantly when tons of bullets are moving simultaneously in the scene.

To switch between the 2 movement modes, simply check useRigidbodyForce to true (for physics-driven bullets) or false (for non-physics). You usually set this in the Editor, during development time.

As you might have guessed, you can set the bullet speed by tweaking the bulletForce variable. For physics-driven bullets, you usually need to set it to a high number, such as 800 or more. For non-physics bullets, set it to a lower number like 10 for smaller scenes like our current one. Remember, the physics-driven force amount will usually be higher than the non-physics movement.

If this script isn't already attached to the Bullet object you created earlier in the scene, attach it now. When you play the scene, the bullet should fly forward without end with the Trail Renderer helping you visualize the bullet's flight:

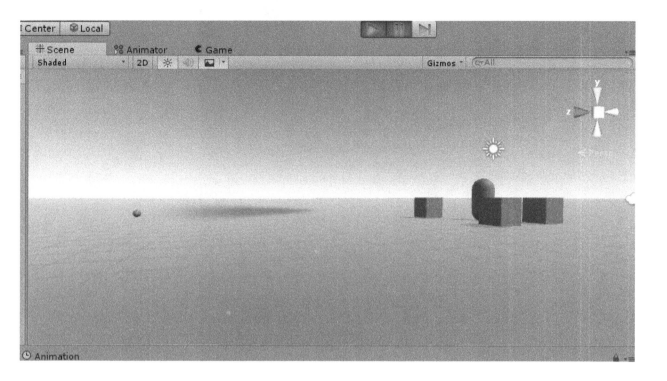

Now it's time to give our bullet the ability to cause damage. We will be using Unity's OnTriggerEnter() method. In the Projectile.cs script, enter the following method and code:

```
void OnTriggerEnter(Collider other) {
    if (other.isTrigger == false) {
            Instantiate(onHitEffect, myTransform.position,
                                          myTransform.rotation);


            if(other.gameObject.GetComponent<Health>() != null){
                    other.gameObject.GetComponent<Health>().TakeDamage(damage);
            }


            DestroyBullet();
    }
```

```
}
```

The OnTriggerEnter() method automatically fires whenever the bullet's collider hits another object's collider, as long as one of the objects has an attached Rigidbody. What this code block does is 3 important things:

1) Spawn the on-hit effect when the bullet collides with an object

2) Send damage to the object's Health component if it has one attached. This uses the public method TakeDamage() that we created in the Health module earlier.

3) Remove the bullet from the scene.

IMPORTANT: Either the bullet or the object it hits must have both a collider and Rigidbody attached. If you have followed the bullet prefab setup completely, you should already have a Rigidbody attached to the bullet object.

If you play the scene, the bullet will fly forward and upon hitting another object, will generate on hit effects and then delete itself. You can test it by placing a wall in front of the bullet, in its forward direction. When you play the scene, the bullet will fly into it and generate sparks, and the bullet object will be gone from the Scene Hierarchy.

We're done with our Projectile.cs script and the final result should resemble this:

14.8 /   PROJECTILE.CS

```csharp
using UnityEngine;
using System.Collections;


public class Projectile : MonoBehaviour {


    public float bulletForce = 10f;
    public bool useRigidbodyForce = false;
    public float damage = 15f;
    public float secondsToSelfDestruct = 5f;
    public GameObject onHitEffect;


    private Transform myTransform;


    void Start(){
        // cache our transform for faster performance:
        myTransform = transform;
    }



    void OnEnable(){
        // Rigidbody Physics mode:
        if (useRigidbodyForce && GetComponent<Rigidbody>() != null){
            Rigidbody r = GetComponent<Rigidbody>();
            Vector3 forwardDir =
                            myTransform.TransformDirection(Vector3.forward);


            // reset previous physics:
            r.velocity = Vector3.zero;
```

```csharp
                        r.AddForce(forwardDir * bulletForce);

        }


        Invoke("DestroyBullet", secondsToSelfDestruct);

}


        void FixedUpdate(){
                // Simple movement mode:
                if (!useRigidbodyForce){
                        myTransform.Translate(0,0, (Time.deltaTime * bulletForce));
                }
        }



        void OnTriggerEnter(Collider other) {
                if (other.isTrigger == false) {
                        Instantiate(onHitEffect, myTransform.position,
                                                        myTransform.rotation);


                        DestroyBullet();


                        if(other.gameObject.GetComponent<Health>() != null){
                                other.gameObject.GetComponent<Health>().TakeDamage(damage);
                        }
                }
        }


        void DestroyBullet(){
                Destroy(gameObject);
        }


}
```

End Code for Projectile.cs

With the Projectile script finished, make sure it is attached to the Bullet object in your scene that you had created earlier in this chapter. To finish, drag the Bullet object into the /Prefabs/ folder to make it a prefab that we will later load into our Ranged attack module.

15 / THE MOVEMENT MODULE

15.1 /   THE BASIC MOVEMENT FUNCTION

The Movement module consists of global functions that allow the agent to move through a game scene. It may optionally contain pathfinding algorithms. Other modules will call these movement functions should they decide to move the agent.

In a 2D game environment, moving an agent is fairly straightforward. Think of the 2D game scene has a very large graph with tiny units. Each point in the game window has an X and Y coordinate (x, y). The x represents your window from left to right and the x is top to bottom. Usually, the top edge of the window is at Y = 0, and the left edge is at X = 0.   So assume your agent starts top left corner (0, 0) and you have 2 variables, x and y. To move the agent 1 step to the right, you would simply do x = x + 1. And to move the agent down the screen, do y = y + 1. The agent's position will now be at (1, 1). To move the agent back up, you would do y = y - 1, ending up at (1, 0). To move the agent across time, you would simply set a speed (in this example, it's 1), and move the agent towards a specific direction on every tick. This is a way of utilizing 2D vectors. Some popular 2D game engines, particularly those aimed at non-coders, simplify this for you, such as the Construct 2 engine.

In a 3D game environment, moving an agent is more complicated, due to the addition of a third variable: z. Movement and direction depend on 3D vectors, which consist of 3 variables: (x, y, z). Building on our 2D example, assume we have a position (x,y) at (0,0), which is the top left corner of the screen. X is left/right, and Y is up/down. In order for it to become a 3D position, we must add the variable z to it, to show its depth going either forward (positive) or backward (negative). So an agent at the top left corner of the screen that is 1 unit away can be at (0, 0, 1). If the agent were to take a step back, it would end up at (0, 0, 0). Similar if the agent jumped on a ledge, it might be at (0, 5, 0). Note that the direction that each variable represents may differ between game engines, as in the case of Unity and Unreal Engine (the Y and Z directions are reversed).

If you're interested not only in game development, but the actual creation your own game engine or framework, then a solid understanding of linear algebra is a must. However, since your primary objective is to develop a successful game that players will love, you need not be concerned with the underlying mathematical theories. In fact, unless you're building an entire game engine, we recommend that you not waste your time reinventing the wheel and instead focus on creating captivating NPC characters, addicting gameplay, and a mesmerizing storyline. Most of the widely used game development tools available today take care of the complicated math for you so you can focus on what's important. Additionally, linear algebra is beyond the scope of this book that is meant to serve as a guide for game

A.I.

Many popular game development tools, such as Unity, Unreal, and CryEngine, already have movement and pathfinding API built-in, in addition to solving complicated mathematical calculations under the hood, without any effort on your part. If you are using a development tool similar to these, the Movement module of your A.I. should consist of functions that use the movement and pathfinding API of your tool.

The two most common methods for moving an agent are simple position translation, sometimes accompanied by obstacle awareness, and using a pathfinding system. The latter method, pathfinding, is a movement system that comprises the following general steps:

> 1. Determine if a path exists between its current location and a destination position, using a pathfinding algorithm. If a viable path exists that isn't blocked by obstacles such as a body of water, buildings, or changes in altitude, then go on to #2.

> 2. Draw a path to that destination and remember that path.

> 3. Move the agent or object along the path until it reaches the final destination point.

A pathfinding algorithm usually calculates the shortest route, though on some occasions the developer may prefer a longer route to simulate less intelligent NPCs. There are many pathfinding algorithms open to public use, with the most popular in game development being the A Star algorithm. We will introduce and simplify pathfinding algorithms in the next chapter.

For now, we will discuss the simplest movement method: position translation. Translation simply modifies an agent's in the game world. For example, say an agent is standing at the center of the world, at X position 0, and Z position 0. He is also standing at ground level, at Y position 0. This agent would have a Vector 3 position of (0, 0, 0). Now, assume there is a target object 5 units to his right, at a position of (5, 0, 0) that the agent needs to grab. You would simply tell the agent to translate his position 5 units to the right to reach the target. Most professional game development tools come with their own basic movement function that automatically translates an object's position for you. If your current tool does not have this basic feature, then we recommend exploring a new tool.

For example, in the Unity engine, you can move an agent forward with this very basic line of code:

```
// "transform" represents the agent
transform.Translate(Vector3.forward * Time.deltaTime);
```

Here, *Translate()* is the function name and *Vector3.forward* represents the direction of travel (in this case, directly forward). Time.deltaTime represents the delta, or change in time, and multiplying the forward Vector by the change in time will allow the agent to repeatedly move forward across game time.

On a side note, to integrate a *speed* parameter into this function, you would simply create a variable *speed* and then multiple that by deltaTime:

```
float speed = 15;
transform.Translate(Vector3.forward * Time.deltaTime * speed);
```

15.2 /   BASIC FORWARD MOTION

Once you become familiar with your development tool's built-in basic movement function, you'll need to integrate it into the agent's Movement module. To do so, you can create a global function on the agent like this:

```
// part of class Agent
public void MoveAgentForward(){
        // .Translate() is a convenient part of the Unity API that
        // automatically moves an object in a specific direction.
        transform.Translate(Vector3.forward * Time.deltaTime);

}
```

Another script or class can now call this function, MoveAgentForward() anytime they wish the specific agent to move forward.

For instance, let's say there are 2 agents in your scene: SQUAD LEADER and ROOKIE. ROOKIE has the MoveAgentForward() function inside of his Movement module. During gameplay, SQUAD LEADER needs to command ROOKIE to move forward anytime he wishes. To do so, SQUAD LEADER simply has to call the public MoveAgentForward() function on ROOKIE.

Specifically in Unity, SQUAD LEADER can command ROOKIE to move forward with the following code:

```
public GameObject squadUnit1;
public GameObject squadUnit2;
public GameObject squadUnit3;


void Command_Squad_To_Charge_Enemy(){
        squadUnit1 = rookie;        // reference to ROOKIE
        squadUnit1.GetComponent<Agent>().MoveAgentForward();


        // if other squad units exist, we can do something similar to them:
        squadUnit2 = rookie2;
        squadUnit2.GetComponent<Agent>().MoveAgentForward();
```

```
}
```

This gives other modules a straightforward and organized way to move a specific agent. Additionally, this helps to keep your code base small, organized, and consistent. For example, assume you suddenly developed a new idea: The agent should also jump each time it moved forward. You would only need to update a single function inside the Movement module, and the agent will perform the updated actions each time it moves, regardless of where the command originated from. Furthermore, multiple entities can command this agent to move using the same function.

15.3 /   BASIC ROTATION MOTION

Knowing the basic movement API for your game engine is useful, however we will not be able to create more advanced moving agents with the basic functions alone. With the basic movement function in mind, we now introduce another building block of motion: Basic rotation functionality. Most popular game engines should already have a basic API that rotates an object, automatically taking care of the math for you. In Unity, there are two basic methods to rotating an object:

Method 1: using transform.Rotate()

```
// transform represents the object in Unity
// this rotates the object towards its right, across game time
transform.Rotate(Vector3.right * Time.deltaTime);
```

Method 2: setting transform.rotation and Quaternions

In Unity, a quaternion represents a rotation and the complex math behind it is taken care of for you.

```
// Here, we smoothly rotate the object (transform) towards a target
// position (targetDir)

// set the target position (direction)
Vector3 targetDir = new Vector3(3, 5, 0);

// get the actual rotation target from our object to the target position:
Quaternion rot = Quaternion.LookRotation(targetDir - transform.position);

// rotate our object towards the rotation target:
transform.rotation = Quaternion.Slerp(transform.rotation, rot,
Time.deltaTime);
```

For the purposes of our A.I., we will be using Method 2. If you're not using Unity, then you must find a similar function for your game engine that allows you to dynamically set the rotation of an object at runtime. The basic flow goes like this:

1. Input a target position, either as a Vector2 or Vector3 position.

2. Convert that position into a target rotation, after subtracting the agent's current position from the target position.

3. Use the game engine's built-in rotation function to rotate towards the target rotation.

4. Stop rotating when the new rotation is reached.

We will use this basic rotation building block to create a function for our A.I. agent that will allow him to automatically rotate towards any given point. This new function will take in a target position, convert the position to a target rotation, and rotate the object towards it. Similar to our movement function, the rotation method is global and can be called by other scripts, agents, and objects. In Unity, we can create a function similar to the following:

```
float turnSpeed = 5;

public void RotateTowardsDest(Vector3 dest){

        Vector3 targetDir = new Vector3(dest.x, dest.y, dest.z);

        Quaternion rot = Quaternion.LookRotation(targetDir -
                transform.position);

        transform_cache.rotation =
                Quaternion.Slerp(transform.rotation, rot,
                Time.deltaTime * turnSpeed);
}
void FixedUpdate(){
        // Fixed Update in Unity happens every game tick

        // here, we will call our new function every tick
        // so that our object can smoothly rotate towards the target across
        // game time

        RotateTowardsDest(new Vector3(5, 15, 30));

}
```

The above code creates a simple turret-like behavior. The object will rotate towards a Vector3 position given in the FixedUpdate() method. You may notice that this will cause the object to completely rotate towards a target position. Thus, if the target position is located above and to the east of the object, it will cause the object to slant towards the east, like an arrow, However, if we apply this to humanoid A.I. agents, their entire body, from head to feet, will rotate towards the target, creating an undesirable and unrealistic effect. Their feet will slant off the ground and their body will point towards the northeast. Instead, we want a humanoid agent to only turn his body left or right, and not up or down, regardless of whether the target position is above or below the agent. To do this, we simply make a small change to the above code:

```
float turnSpeed = 5;

public void RotateTowardsDest(Vector3 dest){
        // we make a small change to this line
        // (everything else stays the same)
```

```
            Vector3 targetDir = new Vector3(dest.x, transform.position.y,
            dest.z);

            Quaternion rot = Quaternion.LookRotation(targetDir -
                    transform.position);

            transform_cache.rotation =
                    Quaternion.Slerp(transform.rotation, rot,
                    Time.deltaTime * turnSpeed);
    }

    void FixedUpdate(){
            // FixedUpdate in Unity happens every game tick

            // here, we will call our new function every tick
            // so that our object can smoothly rotate towards the target across
            // game time

            RotateTowardsDest(new Vector3(5, 15, 30));
    }
```

Basically, we took the target position and created a new target position out of it. This new target position retains the forward/backward and left/right coordinates of the original target position, but uses the object's own Y (altitude) position. This way, the object will rotate towards the target but will now assume that the target is at the exact same height level as itself. This forces the object to only rotate left or right and never up or down.

15.4 /   COMBINING FORWARD MOTION AND ROTATION

With our basic movement and rotation functions developed, we combine them to create a simple motion system that involves a loop comprising the following steps:

1. Receive target's current position

2. Rotate towards target direction (our Rotation function)

3. Move forward (our Movement function)

4. Check target's position again (in case target has

moved)

5. Go back to Step 1

At Step 3, even though the agent is only moving forward, it is in fact moving towards the target because it rotated towards the target's direction during Step 2. If the target moves, the agent will pick up the new position during Step 4 and adjust its rotation as needed.

In a simple game world, the agent will most likely not have any problems reaching its target when using the above formula. However if the game world were to also contain obstacles such as walls, buildings, and props, the agent will need to have obstacle awareness in order to traverse around the obstacles. Without obstacle awareness, the agent might never reach a target on the other side of a wall. We will discuss obstacle awareness in another section but for now, for purposes of simplicity, we will continue our discussion about our simple agent motion system.

The following diagram shows an agent, under no threat, using our simple motion system:

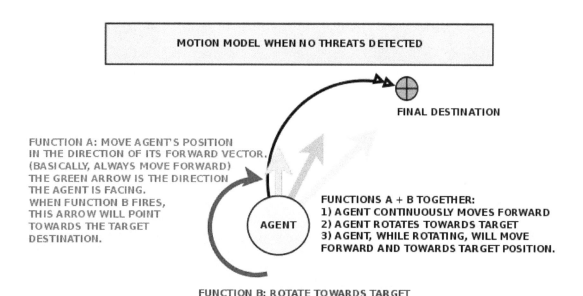

MOTION MODEL WHEN NO THREATS DETECTED

FINAL DESTINATION

FUNCTION A: MOVE AGENT'S POSITION IN THE DIRECTION OF ITS FORWARD VECTOR. (BASICALLY, ALWAYS MOVE FORWARD) THE GREEN ARROW IS THE DIRECTION THE AGENT IS FACING. WHEN FUNCTION B FIRES, THIS ARROW WILL POINT TOWARDS THE TARGET DESTINATION.

AGENT

FUNCTIONS A + B TOGETHER:
1) AGENT CONTINUOUSLY MOVES FORWARD
2) AGENT ROTATES TOWARDS TARGET
3) AGENT, WHILE ROTATING, WILL MOVE FORWARD AND TOWARDS TARGET POSITION.

FUNCTION B: ROTATE TOWARDS TARGET

If the agent encounters a threat and the agent has combat capability, then we will slightly modify the above steps for an alternative action sequence:

1. Receive destination position

2. Detect hostile agent nearby

3. Rotate towards hostile agent (instead of destination position)

4. Move towards destination position (instead of only forward)

5. Fire weapons in forward direction (since we've rotated towards hostile agent) – We discuss combat functions in a future chapter

6. Check destination position again

7. Check hostile agent's position again

8. Go back to Step 1

MOTION MODEL WHEN THREAT IS DETECTED

 FINAL DESTINATION

FUNCTIONS A + B + C TOGETHER:
1) AGENT MOVES TOWARDS FINAL DEST
2) AGENT DETECTS THREAT
3) AGENT ROTATES TOWARDS THREAT
4) AGENT CONTINUES MOVING TOWARDS DEST, NOT THREAT
5) AGENT, NOW MOVING BACKWARDS, FIRES AT THREAT.

THIS IS A BASIC "RUN AND GUN"
MANEUVER. THE AGENT SHOOTS
IN ONE DIRECTION, AND RUNS
IN A DIFFERENT DIRECTION.

**FUNCTION A: MOVE AGENT'S POSITION
IN THE DIRECTION OF FINAL DESTINATION,
NOT THE INCOMING THREAT, EVEN IF
AGENT IS NOT TURNED TOWARDS THE
DESTINATION.**

AGENT

GREEN ARROW: AGENT IS FACING
TOWARDS THREAT, BUT MOVING
IN A DIFFERENT DIRECTION.

**FUNCTION B: ROTATE TOWARDS THREAT,
NOT THE FINAL DESTINATION, EVEN
WHEN WE'RE NOT MOVING TOWARDS
THE THREAT.**

THREAT

**FUNCTION C: FIRE WEAPONS AFTER AGENT
IS FINISHED ROTATING TOWARDS THE THREAT.**

15.5 /   AERIAL MOTION

We had just discussed a basic motion scheme for our agent's Movement module. The basic motion scheme works for most use-cases, especially ground-level agents. For aerial agents, however, we modify the design slightly for more realism and to compensate for the high speeds usually required of aerial motion.

Aerial agents such as passenger planes, hovercars, fighter jets, and space ships most commonly move at significantly faster speeds than ground-based units. As a result,

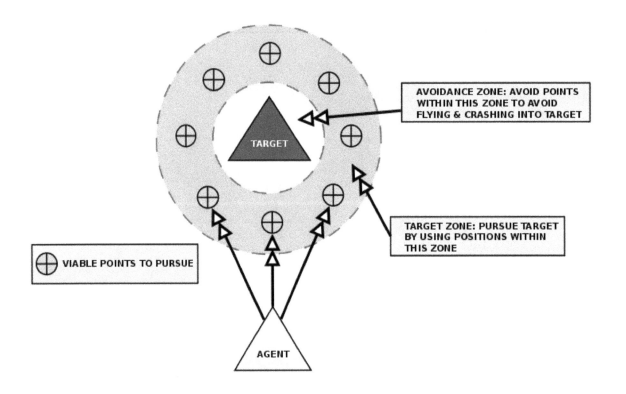

16 / INTRODUCTION TO PATHFINDING

16.1 /   WHAT IS PATHFINDING?

The previous chapter discussed a simple movement system that utilized two basic functions working in unison: A forward-moving method and a rotation function. This chapter will introduce pathfinding and help you to understand it by breaking down complex concepts using a very simple pathfinding method. A pathfinding system uses pathfinding algorithms to determine if a viable path exists between two points – a path that is unimpeded by obstacles. An agent can then use this calculated path as a guide to move through a game world. It allows for more realistic and error-free A.I. movement than the simple motion system we described in the previous chapter. Clearly, pathfinding is very important to game A.I. development and indeed pathfinding systems have been used for decades to power A.I. movements in most commercial games. Thus it's imperative for a game designer to understand what pathfinding is and its significance in developing A.I. agents.

Despite pathfinding's importance, we do not encourage you to develop your own pathfinding system, especially if you are new to game development or don't come from a computer science background. This is because pathfinding is a complex subject – one that encompasses computer science research, patented algorithms and technologies, and a dedicated academic community. The good news is that most popular game engines such as Unity, Unreal Engine, and CryEngine come out-of-the-box with efficient pathfinding systems that take care of the complex search algorithms for you, without much effort on your part. In addition, popular game engine companies have online asset stores, such as the Unity Asset Store, that boast a wide selection of alternative pathfinding systems available to buy or download for free. Thus, if your primary focus is to develop a commercial game and bring that game to market as quickly as possible, it is usually not in your interest to spend ample amounts of time reinventing the wheel. By utilizing built-in pathfinding systems that come with the game engine you're using, your development time spent in the pathfinding area is dramatically reduced to knowing a few simple API commands. Creating a captivating game does not require you to understand how a pathfinding system works, only how to use it. As a result, this chapter will provide you with a introductory and big-picture understanding of pathfinding, by explaining a very simple pathfinding implementation.

As discussed in the previous chapter, an A.I. agent utilizes a pathfinding system similar to the following general steps:

1. Select a destination position.

2. Determine if a path exists between its current location and a destination position, using a pathfinding algorithm. If a viable path exists that isn't blocked by obstacles such

as a body of water, buildings, or changes in altitude, then go on to #3.

3. Draw a path to that destination and remember that path.

4. Move the agent or object along the path until it reaches the final destination point.

A pathfinding algorithm usually calculates the shortest route, though on some occasions the developer may prefer a longer route to simulate less intelligent NPCs. The examples in this chapter focus on finding the shortest route.

16.2 / DESIGNING A SIMPLE PATHFINDING ALGORITHM

So how exactly does a pathfinding algorithm work? How is it possible for a computer to figure out and conceptualize a virtual path from one point to another, taking into consideration every obstacle along the way? There are many approaches to this topic and we will show you a very simple "node-based" implementation.

Imagine a rectangular parking lot holding some cars. How would you get from the START POINT to the DESTINATION POINT?

(See diagram on next page)

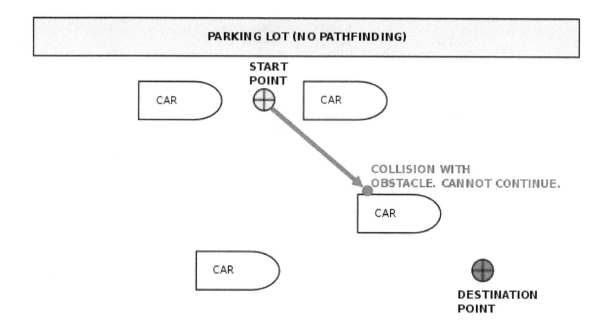

If you, as a human, were to do this, you would walk towards the DESTINATION POINT until you reach the car at the bottom right. Then, you'd proceed to walk around the car before moving again towards the destination. However, if a computer were to do it using a simple motion pattern, it would simple collide with the bottom right car and stop completely, never reaching the DESTINATION POINT. How can a computer find a route *around* the car? The answer is a node graph.

Now imagine you were to cover the entire parking lot with bowling balls. Each ball is placed exactly 10 feet apart. If you were to stand on top of a car and looked down, the scene would look like a loose grid of points. Here, a bowling ball is a node and together they create a graph of the environment.

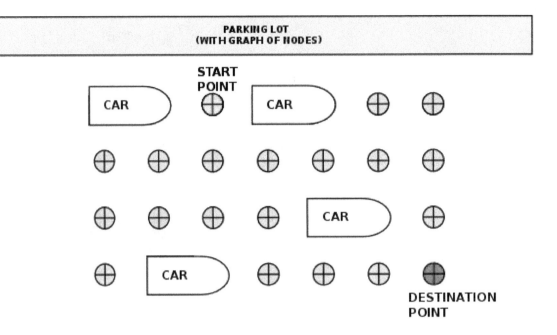

Each blue point is a bowling ball in our example. Each ball, or node, is evenly distributed throughout the environment. A simple pathfinding algorithm that uses graphs and nodes will first generate a graph of the environment in a manner similar to this. Nodes are placed at the lowest ground level and not on top of unwalkable objects. For example, in this case the cars are unwalkable so we lay out our nodes around each car, instead of on top of them. In game development, it's easy to test if a node will drop on a walkable surface or an unwalkable object by the use of raycasts: Simply fire a raycast from a very high level down onto the environment. If it hits a point on the ground or walkable surface, then create a node at that point. Otherwise, do nothing and move onto the next area. The raycasts should be evenly spread out, as in the case of our bowling ball example.

A simple pathfinding implementation would begin at the START POINT and find the next closest node towards the DESTINATION POINT. The algorithm would then loop through every node, checking its proximity to the next and saving the points into memory. The process ends when either the DESTINATION POINT node is reached, or determined to be unreachable. If the destination can be reached, the A.I.

agent will use the list of nodes it saved into memory and move to each, creating a path out of them.

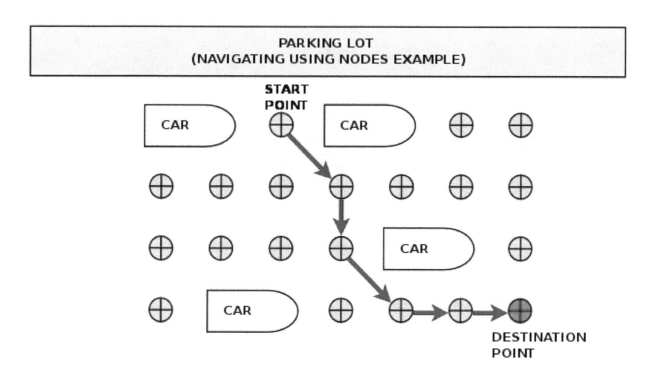

Using a new example, we will now go into detail about how this process works. Imagine a rectangular game map with an A.I. agent and a destination. Like the parking lot example, we overlay a graph of nodes onto the scene. This simple pathfinding algorithm will begin with the agent's starting position and find the closest node. The agent will move towards the closest node. From that point, the pathfinding system will check if a raycast can be fired from that closest node to the DESTINATION node. If so, then a path will be drawn between the two nodes and the system will declare that a path exists.

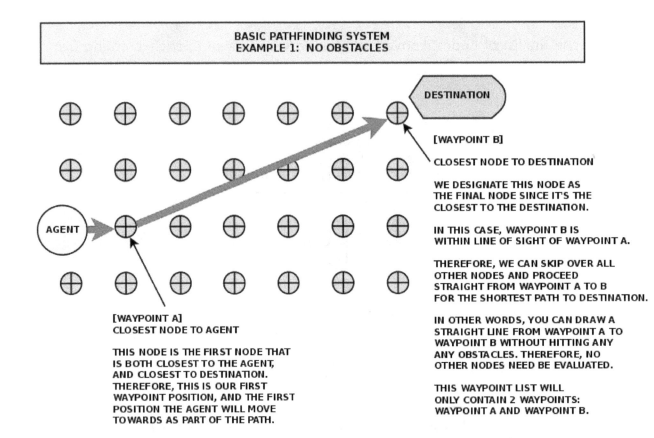

BASIC PATHFINDING SYSTEM
EXAMPLE 1: NO OBSTACLES

DESTINATION

[WAYPOINT B]

CLOSEST NODE TO DESTINATION

WE DESIGNATE THIS NODE AS
THE FINAL NODE SINCE IT'S THE
CLOSEST TO THE DESTINATION.

IN THIS CASE, WAYPOINT B IS
WITHIN LINE OF SIGHT OF WAYPOINT A.

THEREFORE, WE CAN SKIP OVER ALL
OTHER NODES AND PROCEED
STRAIGHT FROM WAYPOINT A TO B
FOR THE SHORTEST PATH TO DESTINATION.

IN OTHER WORDS, YOU CAN DRAW A
STRAIGHT LINE FROM WAYPOINT A TO
WAYPOINT B WITHOUT HITTING ANY
ANY OBSTACLES. THEREFORE, NO
OTHER NODES NEED BE EVALUATED.

THIS WAYPOINT LIST WILL
ONLY CONTAIN 2 WAYPOINTS:
WAYPOINT A AND WAYPOINT B.

AGENT

[WAYPOINT A]
CLOSEST NODE TO AGENT

THIS NODE IS THE FIRST NODE THAT
IS BOTH CLOSEST TO THE AGENT,
AND CLOSEST TO DESTINATION.
THEREFORE, THIS IS OUR FIRST
WAYPOINT POSITION, AND THE FIRST
POSITION THE AGENT WILL MOVE
TOWARDS AS PART OF THE PATH.

This example was very simple because there are no obstacles in the scene. The next
diagram shows what the pathfinding system must do if there is one obstacle on the
map.

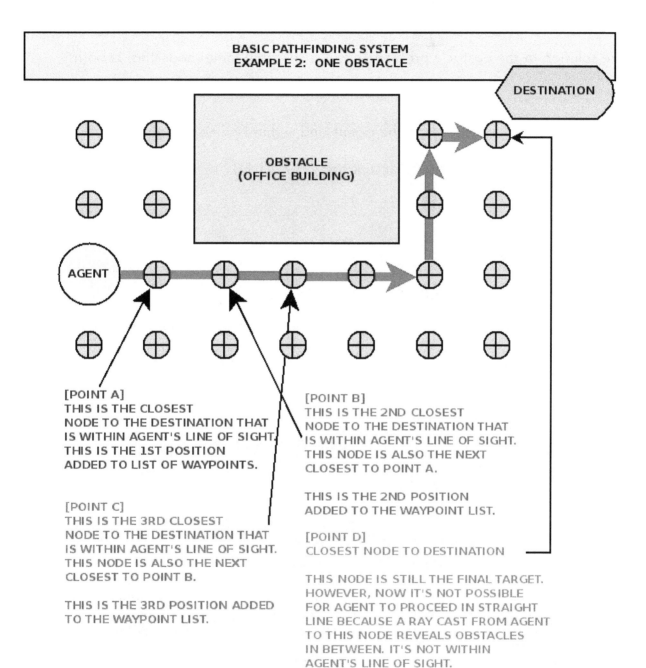

BASIC PATHFINDING SYSTEM
EXAMPLE 2: ONE OBSTACLE

DESTINATION

OBSTACLE
(OFFICE BUILDING)

AGENT

[POINT A]
THIS IS THE CLOSEST
NODE TO THE DESTINATION THAT
IS WITHIN AGENT'S LINE OF SIGHT.
THIS IS THE 1ST POSITION
ADDED TO LIST OF WAYPOINTS.

[POINT C]
THIS IS THE 3RD CLOSEST
NODE TO THE DESTINATION THAT
IS WITHIN AGENT'S LINE OF SIGHT.
THIS NODE IS ALSO THE NEXT
CLOSEST TO POINT B.

THIS IS THE 3RD POSITION ADDED
TO THE WAYPOINT LIST.

[POINT B]
THIS IS THE 2ND CLOSEST
NODE TO THE DESTINATION THAT
IS WITHIN AGENT'S LINE OF SIGHT.
THIS NODE IS ALSO THE NEXT
CLOSEST TO POINT A.

THIS IS THE 2ND POSITION
ADDED TO THE WAYPOINT LIST.

[POINT D]
CLOSEST NODE TO DESTINATION

THIS NODE IS STILL THE FINAL TARGET.
HOWEVER, NOW IT'S NOT POSSIBLE
FOR AGENT TO PROCEED IN STRAIGHT
LINE BECAUSE A RAY CAST FROM AGENT
TO THIS NODE REVEALS OBSTACLES
IN BETWEEN. IT'S NOT WITHIN
AGENT'S LINE OF SIGHT.

THIS IS THE 8TH AND LAST POINT
IN THE WAYPOINT LIST. WHEN WE HAVE
CALCULATED THE POSITION OF THIS NODE,
THE AGENT IS READY TO MOVE ALONG THE PATH.

The solution to the obstacle problem is to first find the initial node that is both:

1. Closest to the agent and within his line of sight.

2. Closest to destination (POINT D)

The first node is POINT A, the first position the agent will move to. The second node will be the closest node to POINT A, that is also closest to the DESTINATION... and so on... until we reach the DESTINATION node. As we find these nodes, each will be added to a list of waypoints. When all positions have been checked and added, the agent will follow each node on the waypoint list in sequential order, like it was moving along a path.

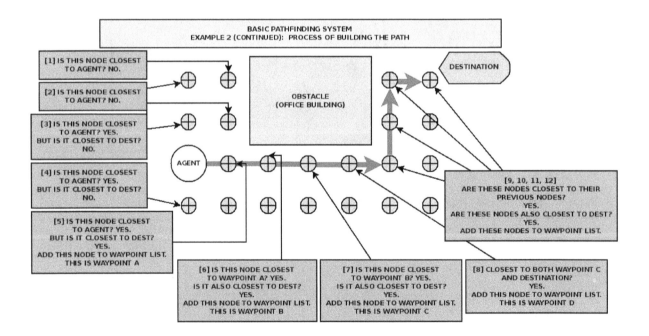

If we were to draw a line through each of the nodes we'd just picked, we'd form a path (red). This is the path the agent will follow to reach the destination.

16.3 / **OPTIMIZING OUR ALGORITHM**

Although we successfully created a path using nodes, it is neither the best nor shortest path. We can optimize this simple example further to shorten the previous path.

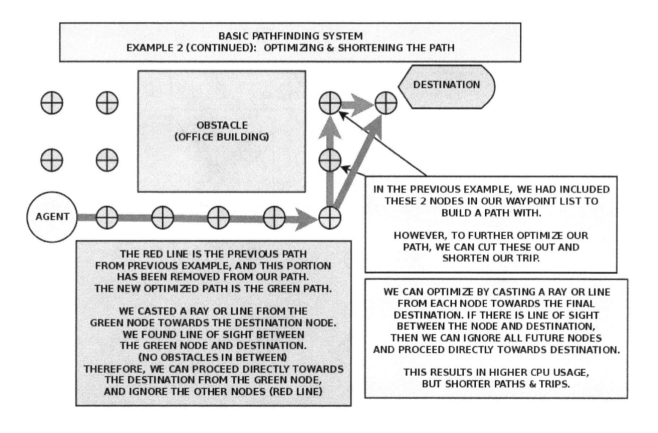

In this new path, we find that we're able to remove two nodes near the end and proceed from the GREEN node straight to the DESTINATION node. How does the agent know that it can proceed from the GREEN node to the DESTINATION without any impediments? We simply fire a raycast from the GREEN node to the DESTINATION node as a test. If the raycast doesn't hit any obstacles along the way, then that tells us that we have a straight path to our destination.

16.4 / **PATHFINDING & TELEPORTATION**

An important scenario to consider is the presence of teleportation devices in the scene. Teleportation devices allow the player to instantly move from one point to another and can be prevalent in science fiction games. In the case that you have such devices in your game scene, a few extra steps must be taken in calculating the shortest path to a destination point.

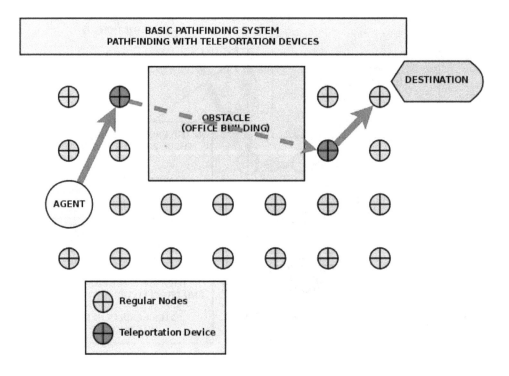

The following is a broad description of the new steps needed when considering teleportation devices:

1. Gather positions of all teleporters in the game scene.

2. Get the closest teleporter from the destination point.

3. Get the closest teleporter from the agent.

4. Add the two distances from STEP 2 and STEP 3.

5. Calculate the normal path (without teleporters).

6. Compare the distances of travel by teleportation and travel without (normal travel path).

7. If the teleportation travel path is shorter, then find a path to the nearest teleporter.

8. After we've reached the teleported and warped to the other side, find a path from the teleport endpoint to the destination.

16.5 /   IF NO VIABLE PATH IS FOUND

When we increase the obstacle size, it's obvious to the human eye that there is no viable path from the Agent to the destination using only the available nodes. But how would a machine know that? The solution is to simply cast a ray or line between the previous node to the next node. If the ray collides with an obstacle, then move onto the next node on the map. If all nodes have been checked and a raycast still touches an obstacle, there the machine can conclude that no path exists between the start point and destination.

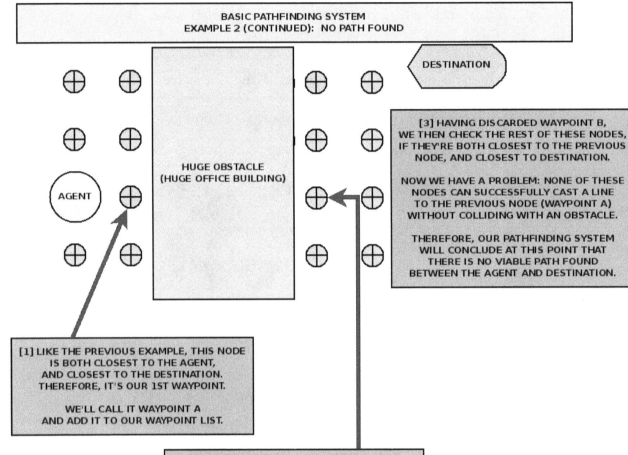

BASIC PATHFINDING SYSTEM
EXAMPLE 2 (CONTINUED): NO PATH FOUND

HUGE OBSTACLE
(HUGE OFFICE BUILDING)

AGENT

DESTINATION

[3] HAVING DISCARDED WAYPOINT B,
WE THEN CHECK THE REST OF THESE NODES,
IF THEY'RE BOTH CLOSEST TO THE PREVIOUS
NODE, AND CLOSEST TO DESTINATION.

NOW WE HAVE A PROBLEM: NONE OF THESE
NODES CAN SUCCESSFULLY CAST A LINE
TO THE PREVIOUS NODE (WAYPOINT A)
WITHOUT COLLIDING WITH AN OBSTACLE.

THEREFORE, OUR PATHFINDING SYSTEM
WILL CONCLUDE AT THIS POINT THAT
THERE IS NO VIABLE PATH FOUND
BETWEEN THE AGENT AND DESTINATION.

[1] LIKE THE PREVIOUS EXAMPLE, THIS NODE
IS BOTH CLOSEST TO THE AGENT,
AND CLOSEST TO THE DESTINATION.
THEREFORE, IT'S OUR 1ST WAYPOINT.

WE'LL CALL IT WAYPOINT A
AND ADD IT TO OUR WAYPOINT LIST.

[2] THIS IS THE NEXT NODE THAT IS BOTH
CLOSEST TO THE PREVIOUS NODE (WAYPOINT A)
AND CLOSEST TO DESTINATION.

WE'LL CALL IT WAYPOINT B.

THE PROBLEM IS, THERE IS NO LINE OF SIGHT
BETWEEN WAYPOINT A AND B.
TRY DRAWING A STRAIGHT LINE FROM
WAYPOINT A TO WAYPOINT B WITHOUT
TOUCHING AN OBSTACLE. YOU CAN'T.
THEREFORE, WE CANNOT USE THIS NODE.
WE DISCARD / IGNORE IT.
LET'S CHECK ANOTHER ONE...

17 / MOVEMENT BY WAYPOINTS

17.1 / INTRODUCTION TO WAYPOINTS

The previous chapter discussed a simple movement system using dynamic pathfinding. However, with dynamic pathfinding, the path that the A.I. takes isn't always the path that we want. In order to have more control over the path, we can use a system of waypoints. A waypoint is simply any virtual representation of a position, 2D or 3D, in a game scene. Thus, a system of waypoints is simply a list or array of each waypoint position. For example, imagine you are creating a racing game that involves bi-directional traffic. The race track is circular and curved on all sides so that it would be difficult for an agent to dynamically select a smooth path to simulate race car A.I. As a solution, we can place many cube objects in a circular fashion in the center of the race track. Together, their positions comprise the waypoint system that the A.I. cars will follow.

A major advantage of using waypoints is that they can be placed into a game scene at design time, giving the game developer full control of where he wants his agents to go, or defining where the agents are allowed to go. In many cases, the developer may place waypoints around obstacles so that agents wouldn't even need to use pathfinding systems to move around.

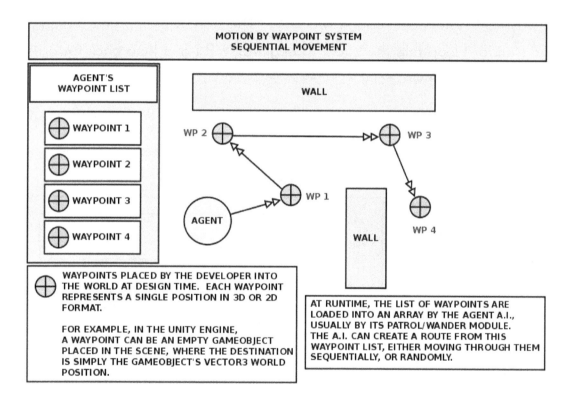

The previous diagram shows a simple, non-looping waypoint system consisting of four waypoints. An agent that processes this system will move towards WP 1 and end up at WP 4, avoiding the wall without further help from another pathfinding system.

17.2 / **STANDARD WAYPOINT LOOP**

A waypoint system can loop in two ways: The standard loop and a ping-pong loop. The standard loop tells the agent to begin at WP 1 and loop back towards WP 1 after reaching the final waypoint.

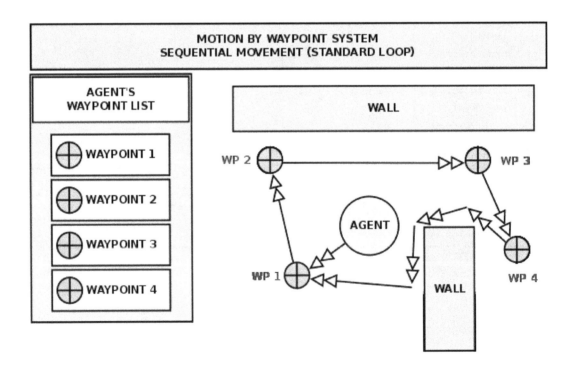

17.3 /   **PING PONG LOOP**

The ping pong loop tells the agent to begin at WP 1 and, after reaching the final waypoint, loop through the waypoints in reverse, starting at WP 3 and moving towards WP 2 and finally to WP 1. This path style is usually referred to a "ping pong" because it resembles a ping pong ball moving back and forth.   In a scripting implementation, you would place the waypoint positions in an array. The agent will begin at array index 0, and end at index 3 (waypoint #4) since indexices begin at 0 instead of 1. As the agent moves through each waypoint, he will retrieve the next waypoint by simply incrementing the index count. Upon reaching WP 4, the agent will move in reverse by subtracting from the index count.

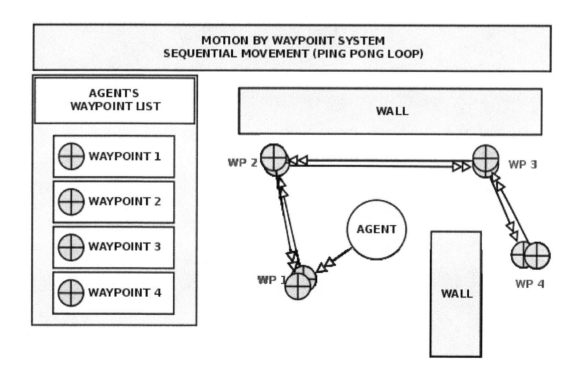

17.4 /   **RANDOM LOOP**

In addition to loops, the agent may be commanded to move through the waypoints in a random fashion. So instead of moving from WP 1 to WP 2, the agent may randomly begin his journey at WP 3 and then to WP 1. This method is useful for simulating random NPC behavior such as a busy town population or dungeon enemies that randomly patrol specific rooms. The random waypoint path may have issues with obstacles since you will no longer have full control over the agent's exact path. While you may have manually placed waypoints around obstacles during design time, the agent may still collide with an obstacle because it is traveling through the waypoints out of order. Thus, random pathing is best used in conjunction with a pathfinding system, in contrast to the two loop styles discussed above which do not necessarily require pathfinding.

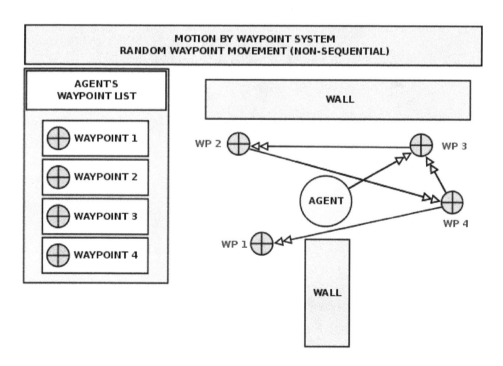

In this example, we assume that we've integrated a pathfinding system along with the random waypoint paths. For example, the agent has randomly selected WP 3 as its initial waypoint destination. The agent will then utilize pathfinding algorithms to move to WP 3. Upon reaching it, the agent will randomly select another point, WP 2 and ask the pathfinding system to calculate a path to that, and so on.

18 / PATROL & WANDER

Patrol and wander agent behavior is can be as simple as an agent following a looping waypoint system, as discussed in the previous chapter, or having the agent move to random positions within its patrol radius.

To show patrol behavior using a simple waypoint loop, we bring back a diagram that was shown in the previous chapter:

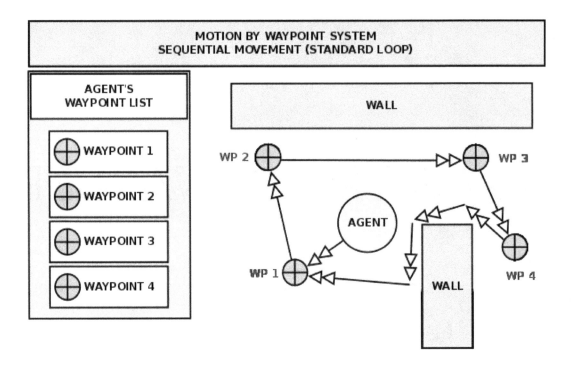

Here, an agent can be given patrol behavior simply by moving from waypoint to waypoint in a sequential loop. These waypoints can be placed at key points in your game that you want patrolled, such as specific dungeon rooms or the boundary of an enemy fortress.

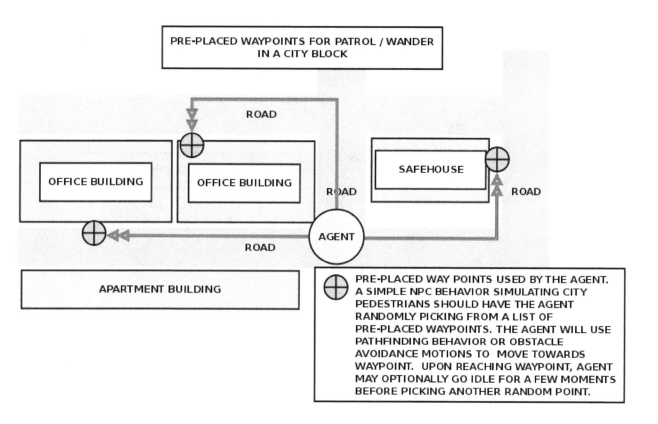

PRE-PLACED WAYPOINTS FOR PATROL / WANDER
IN A CITY BLOCK

ROAD

OFFICE BUILDING

OFFICE BUILDING

SAFEHOUSE

ROAD

ROAD

AGENT

ROAD

APARTMENT BUILDING

PRE-PLACED WAY POINTS USED BY THE AGENT.
A SIMPLE NPC BEHAVIOR SIMULATING CITY
PEDESTRIANS SHOULD HAVE THE AGENT
RANDOMLY PICKING FROM A LIST OF
PRE-PLACED WAYPOINTS. THE AGENT WILL USE
PATHFINDING BEHAVIOR OR OBSTACLE
AVOIDANCE MOTIONS TO MOVE TOWARDS
WAYPOINT. UPON REACHING WAYPOINT, AGENT
MAY OPTIONALLY GO IDLE FOR A FEW MOMENTS
BEFORE PICKING ANOTHER RANDOM POINT.

An effective implementation of patrol behavior is by combining a waypoint system with a pathfinding algorithm. A scenario that would be perfect for this method is the simulation of pedestrians in a city. Waypoints can be manually placed at design time at key locations, such as a safehouse or at the entrance of an office building. Agents may be instructed to randomly move to these waypoints to simulate busy people moving into a house or going to work at the office. Each waypoint position is fed into a pathfinding system each time an agent selects it.

Another method of patrol and wander behavior involves the use of personal wander zones. These zones are established by drawing a circle around the agent. For example, an agent with a wander distance of 5 will have a virtual circle of radius 5 drawn around him. The agent will pick random wander positions from this zone. In this case, the maximum distance to which the agent may wander to will be the agent's current position + 5 units out from that position.

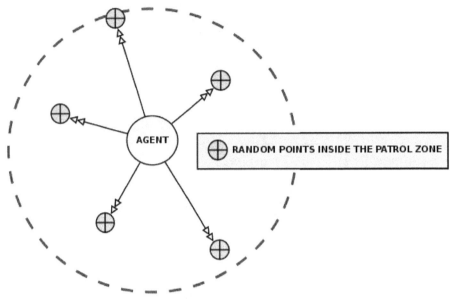

MAXIMUM PATROL / WANDER ZONE

19 / THE DIALOGUE MODULE

19.1 / INTRODUCTION TO AGENT DIALOGUE

Agent dialogue functionality is any capability for an agent to communicate with the human player. This can be any combination of words displayed on the screen, speech audio played through the speakers, or actions and animations played on a virtual character. The dialogue module, then, is is an optional group of functions attached to NPCs that gives them the ability to do just this: communicate with your players. Specifically, the dialogue module consists of a decision-making core that allows an agent to say the appropriate lines at the appropriate time, and a bridge to interface with the game engine's UI or audio system for displaying the dialogue on screen or for playing speech audio.   The module can also be bridged with a text-to-speech system (most Windows, Android and iOS devices have this capability built-in) to dynamically generate audio at runtime.

19.2 /   USING DIALOGUE TO INCREASE IMMERSIVENESS

Communication with players greatly enhances immersiveness and encourages players to become more curious about their environments resulting in a significantly higher level of player satisfaction. Moreover, well-written dialogue can create a degree of immersion that makes players "stick" to a game, possibly for hours on end, never wanting to leave the presence of the facinating virtual characters in your game world. This may be accomplished by:

1. Injecting interesting lore into the dialogue.

BEFORE: [MERCHANT] *"Perhaps I can also interest you in some of my solar weaponry? I have the best prices in town."*

AFTER:

> [MERCHANT] *"You look like the adventurous type! Come. Let us drink to King Elder's recent victory!* **Perhaps I can also interest you in some of my solar weaponry? I have the best prices in town.** *It is said that the Sun-god personally blesses these weapons on the first day of Spring, after Poesidon has ravaged the seas."*

Here, the actual important dialogue is, *"Perhaps I can also interest you in some of my solar weaponry?"* because this is agent is a merchant from which the player may purchase weapons and upgrades. However, that line alone can be quite boring, especially if most merchants in town all say something similar. The trick to reducing boredom and repetitiveness in these kinds of dialogues is to inject lore-related fillers around them.

2. Having companion agents speak at random times during gameplay, using storyline-driven content.

> "Oof! It's really cold out here in the mountains! Hopefully we can retrieve sun stone to heat this place up! " [anticipating future player action]

> "The guards in this city keep looking at me funny. We should go to the merchant to buy some cloaks." [triggers new quest]

> "I heard about the avalanche. [key event that had just happened] Glad you made it back okay."

3. Romance:

NPCs may be given romantic or flirtatious lines to add another layer of immersiveness or to simply enhance the storyline. For example, if an innkeeper in one of your towns is rumored to have a very flirtatious personality, then it would be best for the NPC to actually use flirtatious dialogue. Otherwise, if the supposedly flirtatious innkeeper used boring and bland dialogue, it would decrease immersiveness, realism, and player interest in the storyline. Arguably the most fitting agents for romance purposes are companion agents that follow the player for long periods of time. Be careful, though, because injecting romance into dialogue can be risky; the wrong lines may turn off otherwise excited players who purchased your game for its action-packed gameplay. Always get multiple opinions regarding your character dialogue. Be sure to ask some friends or colleagues to review the dialogue and make sure that none of it is "cheesy."

19.3 / METHODS FOR TRIGGERING DIALOGUE EVENTS

Dialogue events can be triggered using passive or active methods. Passive methods allow NPCs to go on about their business, running through routines and simulating their daily lives. The player must manually activate them in order to trigger a dialogue sequence. In the Unity game engine, an easy way to accomplish this is to raycast a small distance out from the player. If the raycast collides with an NPC, the player may optionally take an action, such as click his mouse, to activate the NPC for speech. Active methods, on the other hand, allow NPCs to initiate dialogue whenever a player moves into its dialogue zone. In Unity, this can be done by creating a trigger collider on the NPC that activates dialogue functions whenever it detects that a "Player" gameobject has moved into its zone. In games such as The Elder Scrolls: Skyrim, a player may move near a villager and that villager will, without any further action from the player, automatically speak such as "good day to you sir!" or "get out of my way!"

19.4 / THE DIALOGUE EVENT ZONE

An NPC running on an active dialogue method has a small dialogue zone around itself. As was just mentioned, this can be done with a trigger collider in Unity. In addition, this can also be accomplished by scripting a small radius around the agent, similar to creating a vision or attack zone.

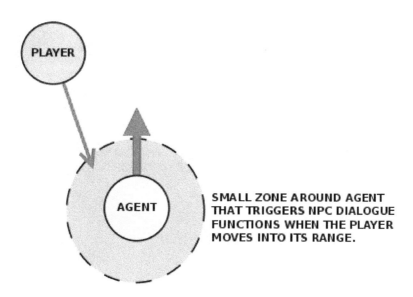

SMALL ZONE AROUND AGENT
THAT TRIGGERS NPC DIALOGUE
FUNCTIONS WHEN THE PLAYER
MOVES INTO ITS RANGE.

19.5 /   EMOTIONAL SCORES

The actual dialogue selected by an NPC can be affected by small variables that represent the agent's emotions or feelings towards the player. A simple example of this is giving every agent a variable called "friendliness" that begins at 0. Each time a player takes specific actions towards the NPC, such as giving him an apple, that variable may be increased or decreased. You can create multiple lists of dialogues, each representing a level of friendliness. For example, the first group of dialogues may only be triggered if the "friendliness" score is from 0 to 19. A second group may represent a "friendliness" score of 20 to 50. A third group with angrier dialogue may represent a "friendliness" score in the negatives, such as -1 to -25. The next time the player interacts with the NPC, it may select a completely new dialogue sequence. This is particularly useful if you have multiple NPCs in a town that are relatively the same unit type, such as guards that all look the same. Giving the guards multiple pools of dialogue to select from, depending on his affinity to the player, adds another dimension of immersion in an otherwise bland scene.

NPCs IN A TOWN CAN HAVE MULTIPLE LEVELS
OF FRIENDLINESS TOWARDS PLAYER.
"FRIENDLINESS" IS SIMPLY A VARIABLE
ATTACHED TO EACH A.I. AGENT THAT TRACKS
ITS FEELINGS TOWARDS THE PLAYER.
CERTAIN EVENTS IN GAME MAY AFFECT THIS VARIABLE.
FOR EXAMPLE, IF THE PLAYER STEALS AN AGENT'S GOLD,
THE ACTION CAN TRIGGER THE AGENT TO SUBTRACT 50 FROM
ITS FRIENDLINESS VARIABLE.

AS A DEVELOPER, YOU CAN USE THIS VARIABLE LATER
WHEN BUILDING DIALOGUE OPTIONS OR A.I. SPECIFIC ACTIONS.

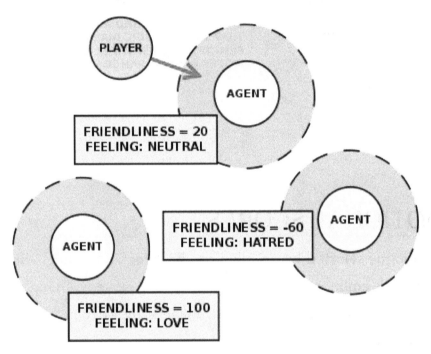

19.6 /   A DECISION TREE FOR DIALOGUE EVENTS

Decision trees become very useful in cases like these. In addition to creating a general pool of dialogue options from which the NPC may select, we can fine-tune the agent's replies based on the player's own responses. This type of dialogue system is often seen in complex RPGs, where the player is presented with several dialogue options, each triggering a different response from an agent.

Shown here is an example of a dialogue system that utilizes a decision tree with multiple options for both player and agent responses, and a "friendliness" variable that dictates how the agent picks his lines.

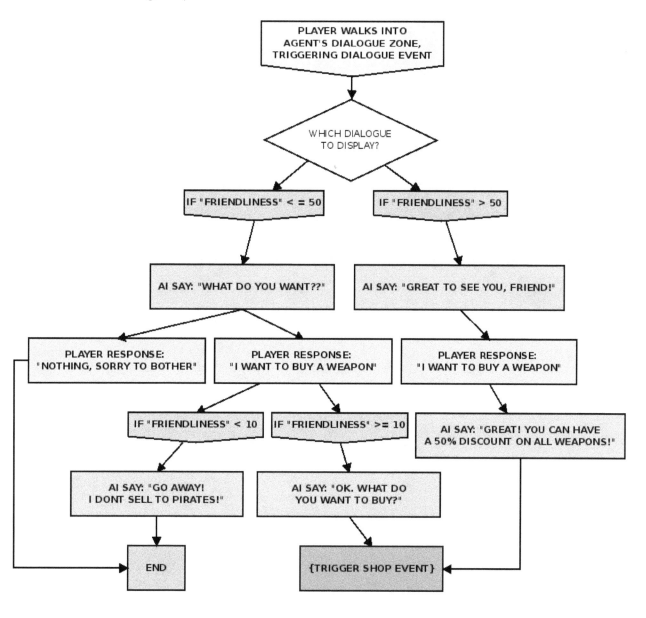

20 / THE SIGNALS MODULE

The Signals Module, not related in any way to dialogue function, allows an agent to communicate with other agents and the human player. It contains a group of global functions that can be called by others to command the agent to perform specific actions. For example, in a squad shooter, the squad leader will use the signal modules of each squad member to direct them to certain locations or specific actions (e.g., opening doors). In a real time strategy game, the player can click his mouse at a point on the screen, sending a message to all the signal modules of every unit to move to that location.

In Unity, the signals module is a script attached to every agent. This script contains global functions, such as "MoveTo()" that can be called by other agents or the player. This function will in turn call the movement functions of the agent's Movement module.

This module is not needed if your game has simple enemies or do not require agents to be commanded by the player or a team leader.

21 / INTRODUCTION TO AGENT TACTICS

21.1 /   THE TACTICS MODULE

The Tactics Module adds extra tactical dimensions to A.I. strategy and consists of pre-configured commands, movement strategies, and formations. This module's purpose is to provide the functions necessary for the A.I. In the upcoming chapters, we will discuss the most widely used tactics in game A.I., including flanking, retreat manuevers, requesting backup, room clearing, and more.

You can think of the tactics module as a sort of reference cookbook for the A.I. agent. It may include recipes for flanking manuevers, calling for backup, and tactical formations. At the right moment, the agent may decide to execute a particular recipe and will refer back to this module for the formula to do so.

The reason agent tactics are placed inside a separate module and not inside the Movement or Combat routines is modularity and code re-usability. For example, assume your game has three units: A tank, an airplane, and a soldier. All three units share the same code for movement. However, you only want the tank unit to have flanking capability, the airplane unit to have both flanking and retreat capabilities, and the soldier unit to have flanking, retreat, and cover-finding capabilities. In this case you would write code for the flanking, retreat, and cover-finding tactics and attach all three to the soldier unit.

You would then simply duplicate the code for the flanking and retreat manuevers and attach them to the tank and airplane units – no additional code needed. In the future, if you needed to create a "lite" version of the tank unit that does not come with a flanking ability, then you'd simply duplicate the original tank and delete the tactics module – no additional code needed.

21.2 /   THE ULTIMATE GOAL OF IMPLEMENTING A.I. TACTICS

The ultimate purpose for implementing A.I. tactics is *not* to defeat your human player or cause him emotional pain, but rather to provide a satisfying, addicting, and rewarding gameplay experience. The key phrase here is "*rewarding gameplay experience.*" While developing A.I. for games, it's easy to get carried away and end up creating A.I. enemies that are too clever and frustrating to defeat. The horror stories of frustrated gamers smashing their keyboards, throwing their Xbox controllers across the room, or leaving disgusted reviews on a game's Steam page are very real. Thus, as an A.I. developer and character designer, you must always remember, during the entire design and development phases, that the purpose of your job is to maximize your players' enjoyment and fun. Whereas the A.I. and tactics used on the battlefields in real life share the goal of absolute victory, the role of game A.I. is to achieve maximum pleasure, regardless of a victory, defeat, or draw.

21.3 /   INTRODUCING BLIND ZONES

Before exploring specific tactics, we must first understand a few prerequisite concepts, mostly to do with zones. Become familiar with the following diagram and take these zones into account when developing combat A.I.

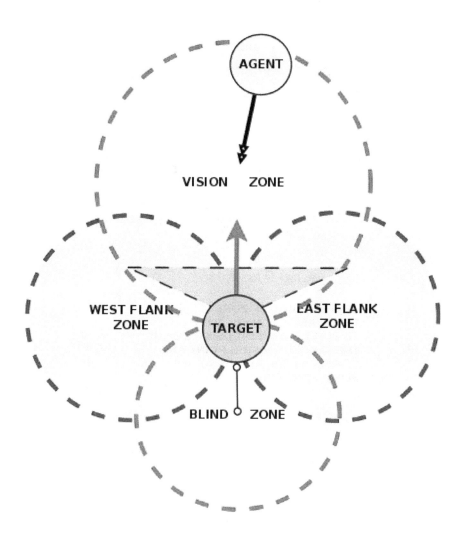

What is a blind zone, and how to represent it in code? The concept of a blind zone in tactical A.I. represents an area that is out of the vision of a target. This target can be a human player or another agent. In code, a blind zone is established by taking into account the target's point of vision, his rotation, and directional heading. The point of vision can be the position of the target's eyes, head, or rotating turret location. More specifically, a blind zone can be created by taking the direction and rotation opposite the target's vision point and adding some distance to that point to create a new point. This distance is the radius specified by the game developer, and the newly created point serves as the center of a circle that represents the blind zone.

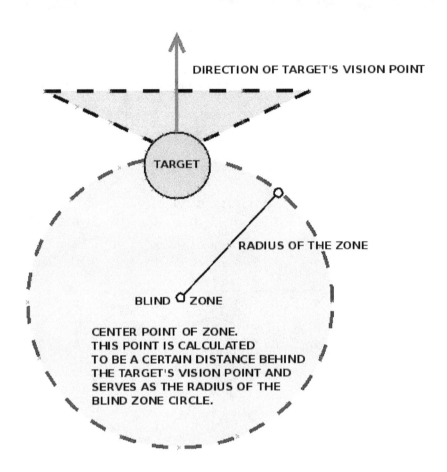

DIRECTION OF TARGET'S VISION POINT

TARGET

RADIUS OF THE ZONE

BLIND ZONE

CENTER POINT OF ZONE.
THIS POINT IS CALCULATED
TO BE A CERTAIN DISTANCE BEHIND
THE TARGET'S VISION POINT AND
SERVES AS THE RADIUS OF THE
BLIND ZONE CIRCLE.

If the target is a tank-like unit, the blind zone will be related to the rotation of the turret itself, and not the tank, unless the tank also has forward vision in addition to rotational turret vision. For this example, we will assume that the target tank's only vision depends on its rotatable turret and where it's scanning.

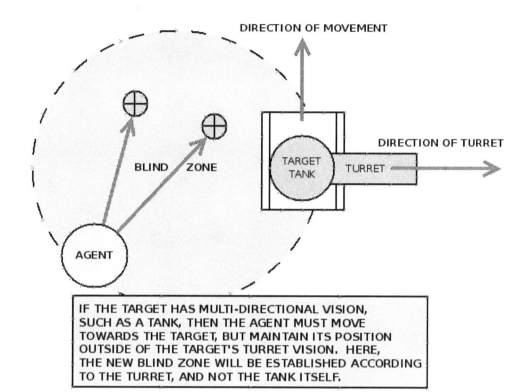

DIRECTION OF MOVEMENT

DIRECTION OF TURRET

BLIND ZONE

TARGET TANK

TURRET

AGENT

IF THE TARGET HAS MULTI-DIRECTIONAL VISION,
SUCH AS A TANK, THEN THE AGENT MUST MOVE
TOWARDS THE TARGET, BUT MAINTAIN ITS POSITION
OUTSIDE OF THE TARGET'S TURRET VISION. HERE,
THE NEW BLIND ZONE WILL BE ESTABLISHED ACCORDING
TO THE TURRET, AND NOT THE TANK ITSELF.

With these zones in mind, the next several chapters will provide a quick general
introduction to the most common tactics used by game A.I.

22 / TACTICS: STEALTH & STALKING

22.1 /   WHY STEALTH TACTICS?

Nothing pushes a player towards the edge of his seat, heartbeat pulsing, back and spine straightened like a monument, and hands sweating at the keyboard than coming face to face with the element of surprise, especially in combat situations. Psychological horror games, such as the Predator alien game series, are famous for their successful execution of horrifying events involving a large alien beast quitely stalking the player through the darkness.

What can be a potentially cinematic and thrilling moment for your players is actually quite simple to implement from a developer standpoint. Two important concepts in implementing a successful stealth agent are keeping out of the player's human vision and maintaining that stealth until the right moment. If the agent jumps out of stealth too early, it may not have the surprise factor you had intended, especially when some clever players had already anticipated a surprise. You must maintain an agent's stealth long enough to create the maximum effect.

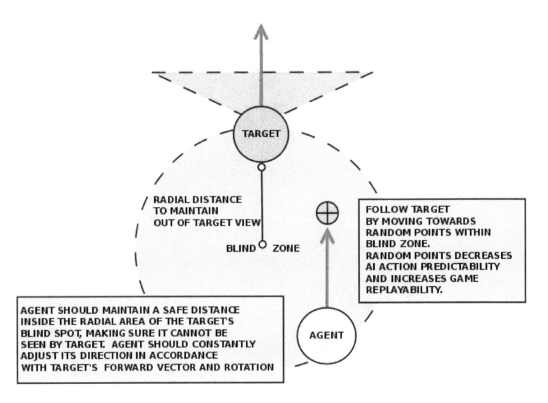

22.2 /   BLIND ZONE SHIFTING

In most cases, a target is sure to move and rotate around the environment. In order to maintain stealth, the game developer must create blind zone shifting to allow an agent to dynamically adjust his position so that he is always inside of the target's blind zone. Blind zone shifting simply involves moving the target's blind zone in accordance with his rotation.

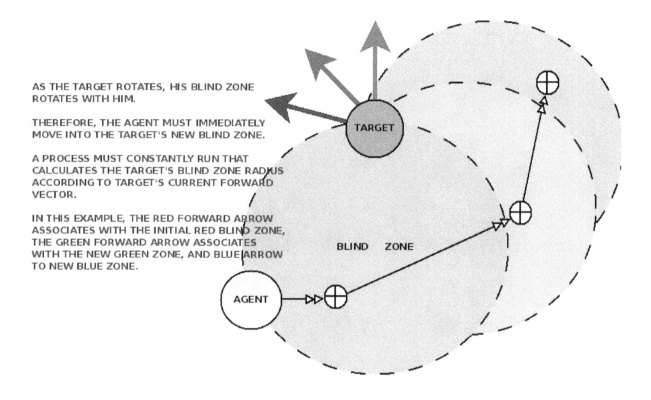

AS THE TARGET ROTATES, HIS BLIND ZONE
ROTATES WITH HIM.

THEREFORE, THE AGENT MUST IMMEDIATELY
MOVE INTO THE TARGET'S NEW BLIND ZONE.

A PROCESS MUST CONSTANTLY RUN THAT
CALCULATES THE TARGET'S BLIND ZONE RADIUS
ACCORDING TO TARGET'S CURRENT FORWARD
VECTOR.

IN THIS EXAMPLE, THE RED FORWARD ARROW
ASSOCIATES WITH THE INITIAL RED BLIND ZONE,
THE GREEN FORWARD ARROW ASSOCIATES
WITH THE NEW GREEN ZONE, AND BLUE ARROW
TO NEW BLUE ZONE.

22.3 / BOXING A TARGET

These concepts still hold if the A.I. element is expanded to included more than one agent. For example, in a three-agent A.I. squad, the team should work to establish a box around the target. The box should be created by agents behind, in front, and at the flanks of the target. Once established, the A.I. may decide to begin an attack or to continue tailing the target.

In the following diagram, all agents seek positions within the target's blind zone, with the exception of AGENT BETA, who is attempting to box the target from the front. Random points are picked from within the blind zone radius to decrease gameplay predictability.

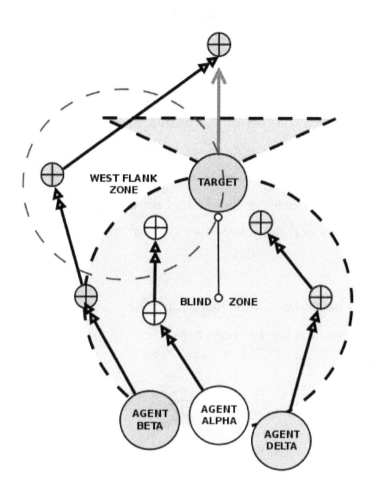

AGENT BETA serves two important roles:

1. Tactical advantage: Moving into the target's western flank gives the squad multiple points of attack and cover.

2. Deception: The agent can move forward, from the western flank, into the target's vision zone. The target, such as a human player, will become distracted by AGENT BETA and will move in to engage. The target will not notice the rest of the hostile squad moving in to attack from his rear. Surprises like these greatly enhance gameplay and if the human player is successful in fending off such an attack, he should feel an elevated level of satisfaction and heightened emotional states.

And, it should be obvious, that increasing the number of agents in a squad, such as this four-agent team example, will give them higher success in boxing in a target:

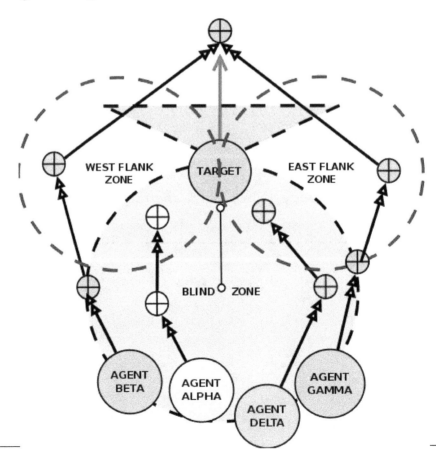

23 / TACTICS: MOVING TO COVER

Cover-finding A.I. tactics help agents seek cover from incoming enemy fire and other dangerous elements within a game's environment. On the screen, agents that take cover when players shoot at them can appear quite impressive and greatly adds to the realism and immersion. For the developer, implementing a cover system can actually be quite simple, depending on how complex your A.I. is.

(See diagram on next page)

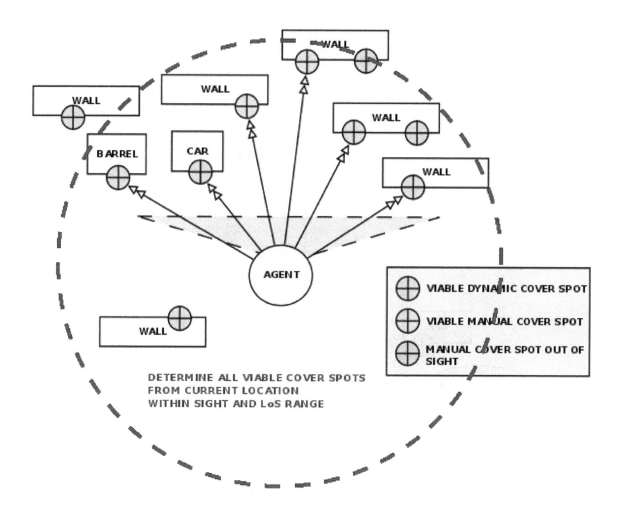

DETERMINE ALL VIABLE COVER SPOTS
FROM CURRENT LOCATION
WITHIN SIGHT AND LoS RANGE

There are two types of cover spots: Manually-placed cover positions marked by the developer, and dynamic cover positions determined by the agent at runtime. A cover system that uses only manually-placed cover spots is the easiest to implement. The developer simply places waypoints at strategic positions, such as behind walls, trees, barrels, etc... At runtime, the agent will constantly loop through the list of manually-placed cover spots and, when it detects one nearby, will move towards it.

Dynamic cover spots are slightly more difficult to implement and harder to get the right effect with. To dynamically find cover spots, the agent must constantly fire raycasts in multiple directions from his position, at varying heights. It's expected that the raycasts will hit nearby objects, such as walls, barrels, and trees. When such objects are detected, the agent will decide the best to move towards, factoring in proximity, direction of incoming hostiles, and direction of incoming fire. The best cover system is one that utilzizes both manually-placed and dynamic cover spots, with manually-placed spots having higher priority during selection.

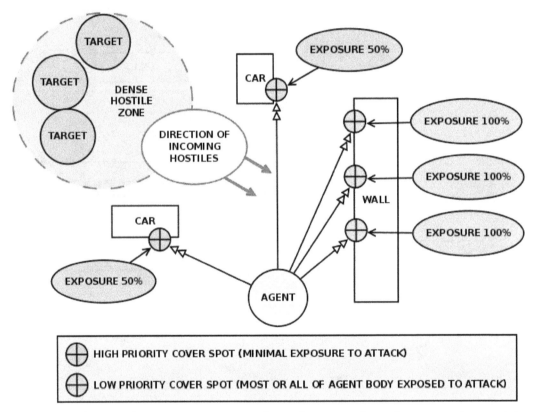

A more advanced cover system involves the use of an "exposure" variable. This variable is a percentage ranging from 0 to 100 that describes the degree of exposure the agent will have to incoming hostiles if the agent were to select a cover spot. In Unity, this exposure variable can be calculated by temporarily copying the agent to a cover position and firing multiple raycasts towards incoming hostiles to check for collisions. For example, in the diagram on the next page, the exposure level from the wall to the incoming hostiles is 100% because multiple raycasts can be fired from those points and connect with the enemies. On the other hand, the exposure level behind the car is only 50%, because a raycast fired at waist-level of the agent towards the incoming hostiles will not collide with them, but another raycast fired from the head of the agent will, since the agent's head is peering over the car.

24 / TACTICS: FLEEING

Agents that have flee behavior should take into account his own health and the ratio of enemies to allies in the nearby area. When the ratio is at a certain level, the agent should move towards the general opposite direction of incoming enemies.

Each agent should have a dynamic retreat zone, that is established by a radius. This area contains all the points from which an agent will randomly pick a location to retreat to.

(See diagram on next page)

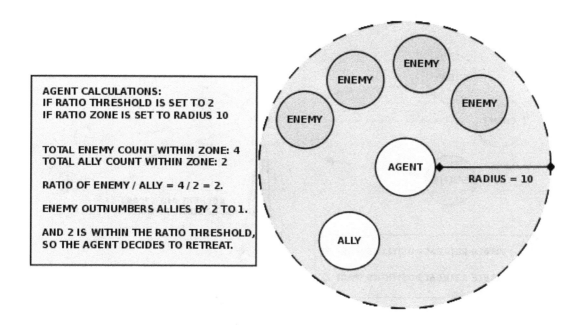

AGENT CALCULATIONS:
IF RATIO THRESHOLD IS SET TO 2
IF RATIO ZONE IS SET TO RADIUS 10

TOTAL ENEMY COUNT WITHIN ZONE: 4
TOTAL ALLY COUNT WITHIN ZONE: 2

RATIO OF ENEMY / ALLY = 4 / 2 = 2.

ENEMY OUTNUMBERS ALLIES BY 2 TO 1.

AND 2 IS WITHIN THE RATIO THRESHOLD,
SO THE AGENT DECIDES TO RETREAT.

After selecting a retreat position and reaching it, the agent may create a new retreat zone and continue selecting random retreat positions away from approaching hostiles, until he can no longer detect nearby enemies.

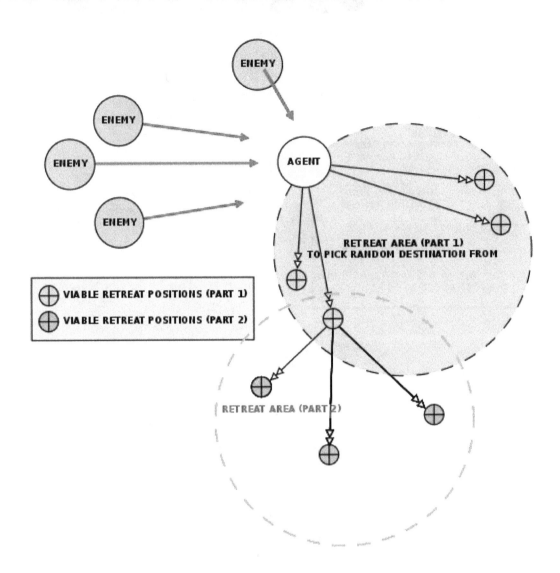

An example decision tree for a flee implementation is shown in the following diagram.

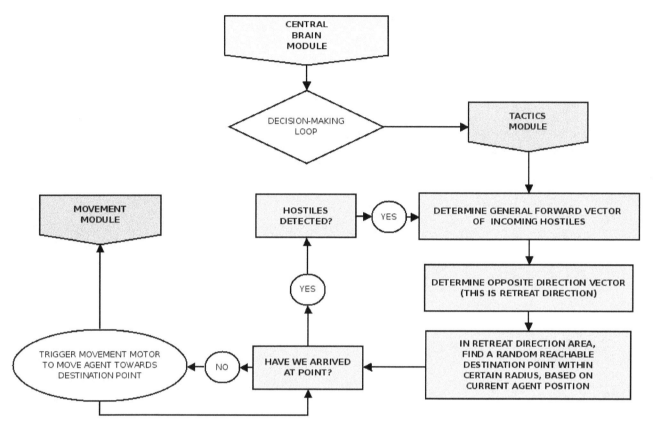

25 / TACTICS: FLANKING

In a previous chapter, we discussed a squad boxing in a target, with one of the squad members moving towards the target's flank. Here, we discuss a similar concept, one that involves a full on flank attack.

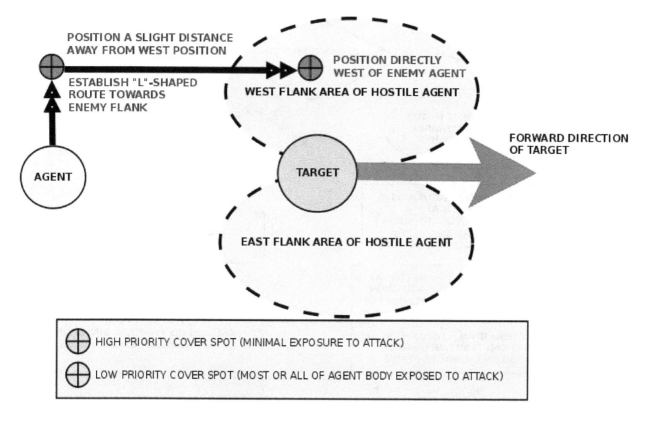

POSITION A SLIGHT DISTANCE
AWAY FROM WEST POSITION

ESTABLISH "L"-SHAPED
ROUTE TOWARDS
ENEMY FLANK

POSITION DIRECTLY
WEST OF ENEMY AGENT

WEST FLANK AREA OF HOSTILE AGENT

AGENT

TARGET

FORWARD DIRECTION
OF TARGET

EAST FLANK AREA OF HOSTILE AGENT

HIGH PRIORITY COVER SPOT (MINIMAL EXPOSURE TO ATTACK)

LOW PRIORITY COVER SPOT (MOST OR ALL OF AGENT BODY EXPOSED TO ATTACK)

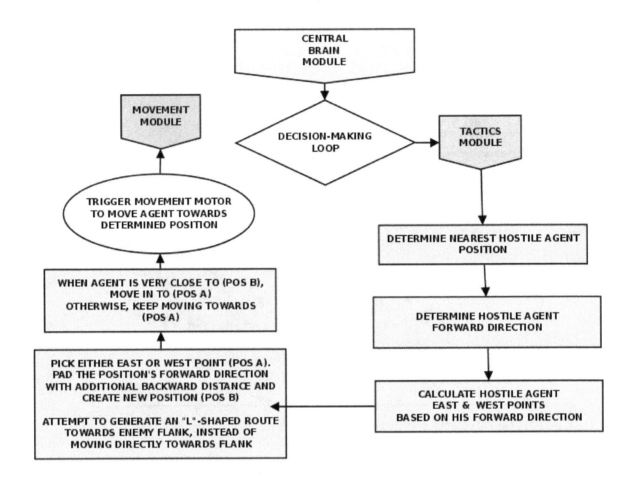

If a squad must approach a target from the front, it is still possible to set up position behind and on the flanks of the target. Instead of engaging the target head-on, the squad should spread out towards the target's flank zones. Some agents will proceed from the flank zone towards the target's blind zone. A single target can only track 1 or 2 objects simultaneously. Therefore, there is a high chance that a forward-approaching squad can sneak move into position inside a target's blind zone without incident.

This maneuver gives several tactical advantages:

1. Disruption: By spreading out units, the target's original intended movement objective can be disrupted as he will now have to maneuver himself to engage the squad.

2. Fire Dispersion: The target no longer has a single area to aim at – he must fire at many directions when engaging the squad.

3. Anti-AOE (Anti Area of Effect) Weaponry: Like #2, if the target is wielding a weapon that causes damage over a large area, such a weapon loses its AOE (Area of Effect) advantages when the squad is spread out.

4. Flanking: Spreading out the squad gives each individual member a chance to flank the target. This chance is aggregated by each squad member.

(See next page for diagram)

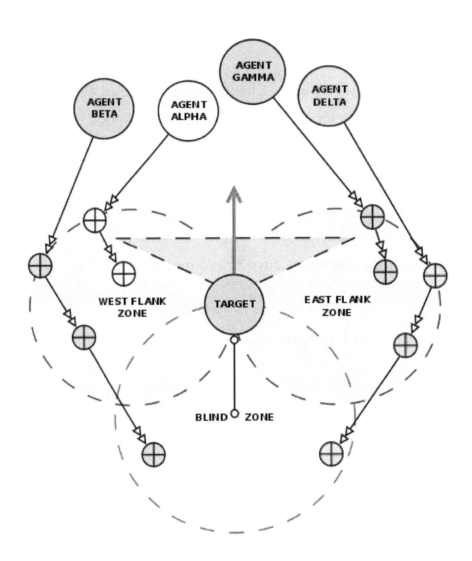

26 / TACTICS: REQUESTING BACKUP

Sometimes an agent must request backup when he is overwhelmed by enemy forces, or low on health. Implementing backup request functionality into the game A.I. is quite simple. To implement requesting backup on low health, the agent should periodically check his health percentage by dividing his current remaining health by his starting health. When the health is below a certain percentage, say 50%, then call the request backup function. To implement requesting backup when outnumbered by the enemy, the agent must periodically check the ratio of nearby enemy to ally units by dividing enemy count by ally count. If the ratio is above a certain level, say 0.5, then call for backup.

A way to determine the quantity and ratio of nearby enemy and ally units is to first tag each unit with a faction tag. In Unity, this can be done simply by setting the unit's tag to a faction such as "Team3". Then, at runtime, loop through every unit in the game scene and check if its tag matches either the enemy or ally team, and place each unit into a team array. Finally, pick a radius around the agent and loop through each unit in the enemy team array, checking if its distance to the agent is within the set radius. If the checked enemy unit is within the radial zone, increase the nearby enemy count by 1. In parallel, do the same with the ally team array, looping through each unit to determine if its position is within the radial zone. Finally, divide the enemy team count by the ally team count to get the ratio. If the ratio is above 1, then enemies outnumber allies; if below 1 then allies outnumber enemies. At a certain level, trigger the backup request function. For example, if there are 4 nearby enemies and 1 nearby ally, then the ratio of enemies to allies is 4 divided by 2. Why 4 divided by 2, instead of 4 divided by 1? Because the agent himself is on the same team as the ally unit, so even though there is 1 ally nearby, there are 2 total agents on that specific team. 4 divided by 2 is 2, which means that enemies outnumber allies by 2 to 1 in this case.

The actual requesting backup function utilizes the Signals module on all ally units. It should simply loop through each unit on the ally team array and send the same Move command to its Signals module with the agent's current position. Consequently, each ally unit will move towards the agent's location.

The following diagram visualizes the radial zone around the agent from which to measure the distances of nearby enemy and ally units.

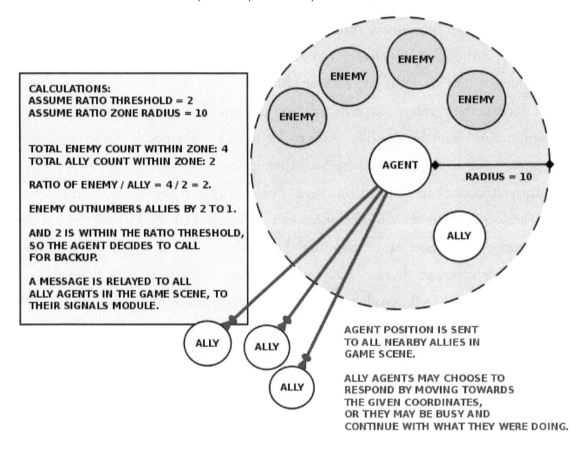

CALCULATIONS:
ASSUME RATIO THRESHOLD = 2
ASSUME RATIO ZONE RADIUS = 10

TOTAL ENEMY COUNT WITHIN ZONE: 4
TOTAL ALLY COUNT WITHIN ZONE: 2

RATIO OF ENEMY / ALLY = 4 / 2 = 2.

ENEMY OUTNUMBERS ALLIES BY 2 TO 1.

AND 2 IS WITHIN THE RATIO THRESHOLD,
SO THE AGENT DECIDES TO CALL
FOR BACKUP.

A MESSAGE IS RELAYED TO ALL
ALLY AGENTS IN THE GAME SCENE, TO
THEIR SIGNALS MODULE.

RADIUS = 10

AGENT POSITION IS SENT
TO ALL NEARBY ALLIES IN
GAME SCENE.

ALLY AGENTS MAY CHOOSE TO
RESPOND BY MOVING TOWARDS
THE GIVEN COORDINATES,
OR THEY MAY BE BUSY AND
CONTINUE WITH WHAT THEY WERE DOING.

27 / TARGET PRIORITIZATION

Target prioritization in game A.I. deals with how an agent decides the order in which to engage hostile units or important objects. While most NPCs in popular games simply target the *nearest* hostile object, giving an agent the ability to prioritize targets not based simply on proximity makes for more interesting battles.

The easiest target prioritization method is by way of utilizing *weights*. A *weight* is simply a number assigned to an object in the game, such as enemy agents, props, weapon pickups, hostages, etc... There is no limit on the range of a weight – it can be 0.2, 1.5, -15, or as high as 5000. During the target selection process, an agent will use the weights assigned to nearby enemies to determine his next target. In addition, the agent will check the weights of nearby objects, such as the enemy flag in a capture-the-flag game, to determine if he should engage nearby targets of lesser weight, or move towards the flag object of higher weight.

Shown: Targeting explosive barrels using weights

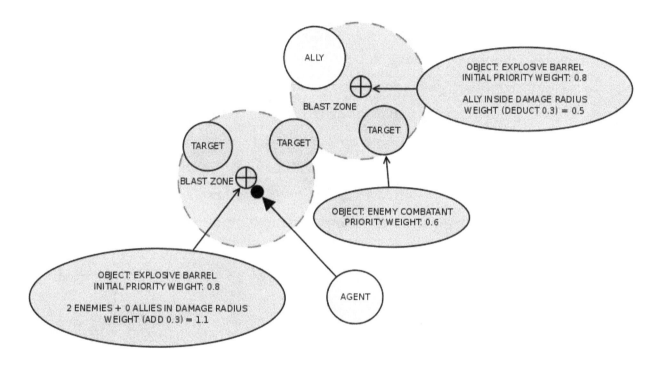

A simple way to imagine weights is to picture a real life scenario on the battlefield. A soldier, armed with a rocket launcher, spots 3 incoming hostiles: A tank, an infantry trooper, and a truck. His commander instructs him to "attack the greatest threat." Using the concept of weights, the soldier determines that the tank is not only the heaviest unit, but also the greatest threat in terms of armor and weaponry. As a result, the soldier engages the tank with his rocket launcher.

Weights are very straightforward to implement with most popular game development tools. For example, in the Unity Engine, a weight can be assigned to an object simply by attaching a variable such as "weight" onto a Game Object. This object can be tagged with a descriptive name such as "Enemy Team" or "Weapon prop". An agent can then loop through all objects of a particular tag, check if they're nearby, and note their weight. As the agent notes the weight of each object he checks, he compares the weight to the previous object. If the current object's weight is higher, then he stores this weight and a reference to that object in memory, before moving onto the next. After he has checked all nearby objects, he engages the one with the most weight.

Weights do not always have to be an additional variable. Often, a weight already exists on an object and can be used during an agent's decision-making process. In fact, all numeric variables attached to an object or another agent can be used as weights. For example, assume an agent's tactical command is to engage the enemy agent with the least health. In this case, the weight is the health variable. The agent will loop through the health levels of every nearby hostile unit, determining the unit with the least health. In another example, assume an agent is instructed to attack the enemy unit that does the most damage. Here, weapon damage variables become the weights. The agent will loop through every nearby enemy and check the damage amount of their weaponry.

As you can see, the simple concept of *weights* opens the door to a plethora of interesting tactical situations for game A.I. Squad shooters can use weights to simulate more realistic squad control. Real time strategy war games can use weights to allow the player to give complex commands to his units. Tower defense games can employ weights to build interesting tower units that attack specific enemy sizes or types. In sports games, such as hockey, the hockey puck can be assigned a weight, the goalie can be assigned a weight, the offensive players and defensive players can be assigned weights, and so on. Each weight helps the agents on both teams to determine their next movement destination and action priorities.

28 / TACTICS: ROOM CLEARING

28.1 /   ROOM CLEARING TECHNIQUES

Room clearing behavior allows agents to automatically enter a room, move to cover and fire positions, and eliminate hostile units inside the room.   Room clearing looks impressive on the screen to players and can greatly enhance the realism of a shooter game. Such behavior is prevalent in first person shooters such as the Call of Duty and the Rainbow Six series, tactical shooters, certain RPG action games, and squad-based real time strategy.   This chapter introduces you to a simple room clearing design that can be easily implemented in most game engines.

Implementing such a system consists of building the room itself, determining the best locations in the room to move to after the door is breached, and loading the interior locations into the agent.

Assuming we have a basic rectangular room with closed walls and a single door, the basic process of implementing a room clearing system is as following:

1. Place waypoints at each corner of the room.

2. Attach a script to the door that contains a list or array of the waypoints from Step 1.

3. Attach a script to the agent that detects when the agent moves near a door. When the agent is near a door, select a random room waypoint from the door, open the door, and move directly to the selected waypoint (in this case, a corner in the room). The agent can be instructed to turn and shoot at nearby enemies during its transit to the waypoint.

This diagram shows the interior waypoint setup that the game designer should take for a basic rectangular room:

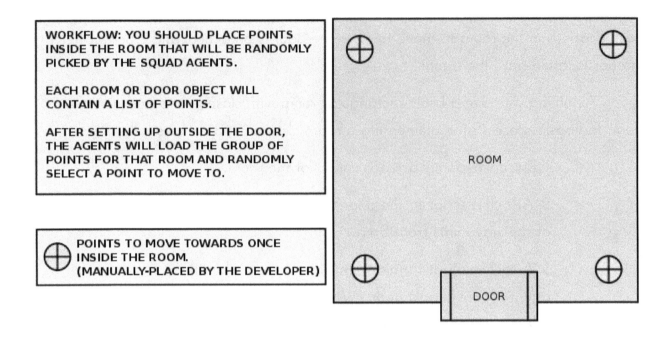

WORKFLOW: YOU SHOULD PLACE POINTS INSIDE THE ROOM THAT WILL BE RANDOMLY PICKED BY THE SQUAD AGENTS.

EACH ROOM OR DOOR OBJECT WILL CONTAIN A LIST OF POINTS.

AFTER SETTING UP OUTSIDE THE DOOR, THE AGENTS WILL LOAD THE GROUP OF POINTS FOR THAT ROOM AND RANDOMLY SELECT A POINT TO MOVE TO.

POINTS TO MOVE TOWARDS ONCE INSIDE THE ROOM.
(MANUALLY-PLACED BY THE DEVELOPER)

ROOM

DOOR

An agent that breaches the door will randomly pick one of the green waypoints to move to, while shooting at any nearby enemies. The door object should have attached scripts with the following design:

THE DOOR CLASS AND COMPONENTS

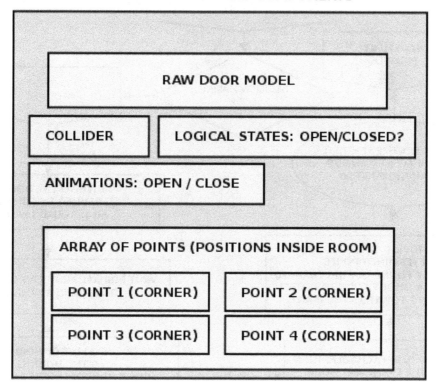

28.2 /   A DECISION TREE FOR CLEARING ROOMS

Specifically, an agent will utilize a similar decision tree such as the one shown in the following diagram:

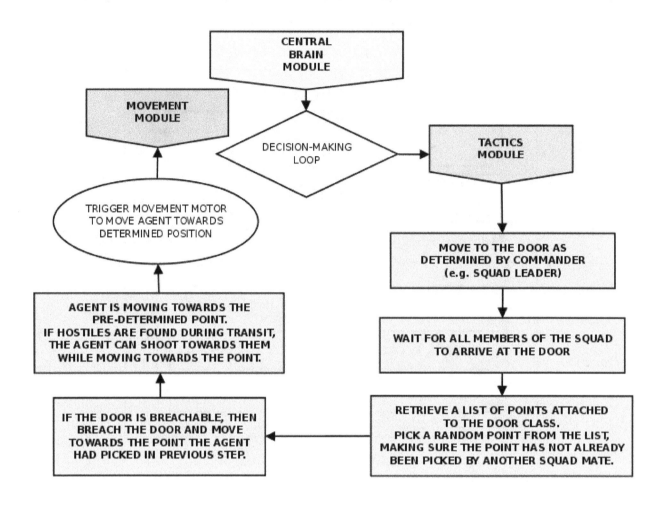

28.3 / CLEARING A RECTANGULAR ROOM

The next few diagrams illustrate a general room clearing scenario with a simple rectangular room.

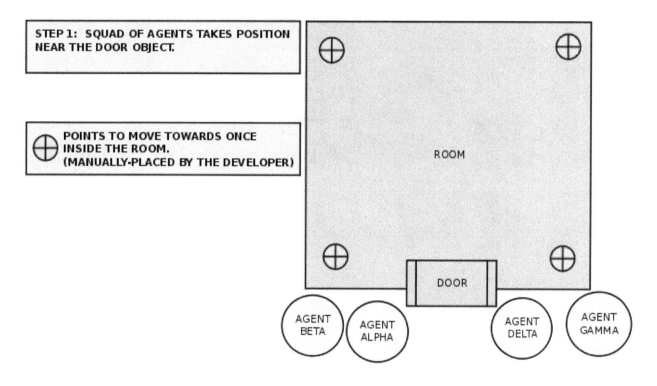

STEP 2: EACH AGENT PICKS A RANDOM POINT INSIDE THE ROOM, THAT HASN'T BEEN PICKED BY ANOTHER AGENT.

POINTS TO MOVE TOWARDS ONCE INSIDE THE ROOM.
(MANUALLY-PLACED BY THE DEVELOPER)

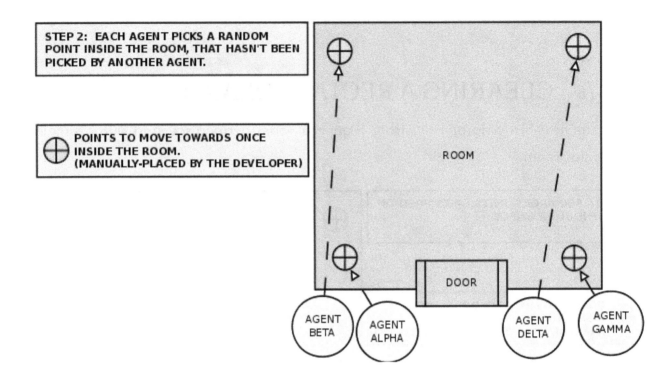

ROOM

DOOR

AGENT BETA

AGENT ALPHA

AGENT DELTA

AGENT GAMMA

STEP 3: AGENTS MOVE INTO THE ROOM, TOWARDS THEIR DETERMINED POINTS.

POINTS TO MOVE TOWARDS ONCE INSIDE THE ROOM.
(MANUALLY-PLACED BY THE DEVELOPER)

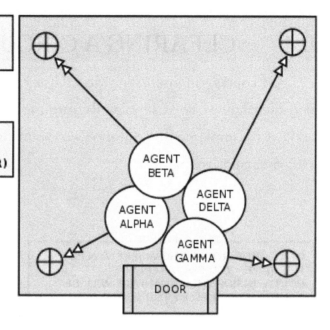

STEP 4: AFTER ARRIVING AT THEIR POINTS, AGENTS ROTATE, SCANNING FOR HOSTILE TARGETS.

POINTS TO MOVE TOWARDS ONCE INSIDE THE ROOM.
(MANUALLY-PLACED BY THE DEVELOPER)

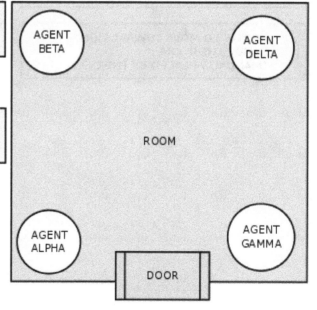

28.4 /   CLEARING A CIRCULAR ROOM

Of course, an interesting game has rooms of many shapes and sizes, not all being rectangular or as simple. Regardless of the size or shape of the room, the workflow for implementing interior waypoints is the same. For example, this diagram shows a circular room:

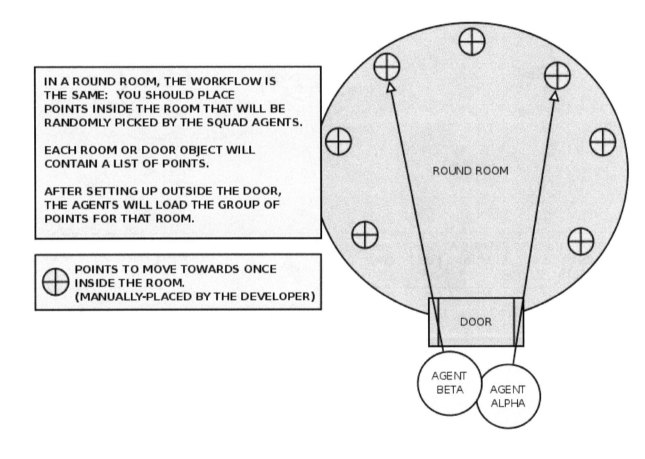

IN A ROUND ROOM, THE WORKFLOW IS
THE SAME: YOU SHOULD PLACE
POINTS INSIDE THE ROOM THAT WILL BE
RANDOMLY PICKED BY THE SQUAD AGENTS.

EACH ROOM OR DOOR OBJECT WILL
CONTAIN A LIST OF POINTS.

AFTER SETTING UP OUTSIDE THE DOOR,
THE AGENTS WILL LOAD THE GROUP OF
POINTS FOR THAT ROOM.

POINTS TO MOVE TOWARDS ONCE
INSIDE THE ROOM.
(MANUALLY-PLACED BY THE DEVELOPER)

ROUND ROOM

DOOR

AGENT
BETA

AGENT
ALPHA

28.5 /   CLEARING A PROCEDURALLY-GENERATED ROOM

If your environments use procedurally generated rooms, then you cannot place waypoints at design time In this case, you must script the A.I. to pick random or strategic points near the corner and long the edges of the room at runtime, based on the general size and shape of the room.

The following diagram shows the waypoint setup for a simple procedurally generated room.

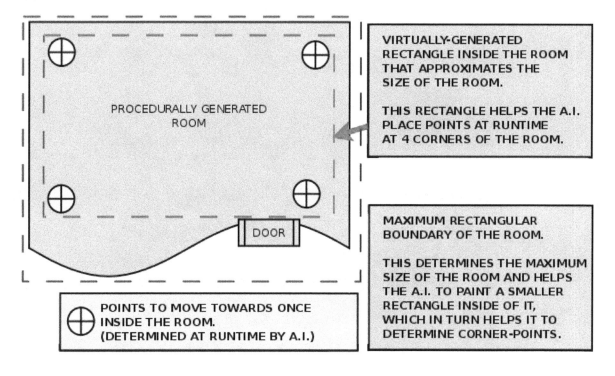

PROCEDURALLY GENERATED ROOM

DOOR

VIRTUALLY-GENERATED RECTANGLE INSIDE THE ROOM THAT APPROXIMATES THE SIZE OF THE ROOM.

THIS RECTANGLE HELPS THE A.I. PLACE POINTS AT RUNTIME AT 4 CORNERS OF THE ROOM.

MAXIMUM RECTANGULAR BOUNDARY OF THE ROOM.

THIS DETERMINES THE MAXIMUM SIZE OF THE ROOM AND HELPS THE A.I. TO PAINT A SMALLER RECTANGLE INSIDE OF IT, WHICH IN TURN HELPS IT TO DETERMINE CORNER-POINTS.

POINTS TO MOVE TOWARDS ONCE INSIDE THE ROOM. (DETERMINED AT RUNTIME BY A.I.)

Since there is no way of knowing the exact corners of such a room at design time, you must estimate the length and width of the room and their corner locations. Procedurally-generated rooms are more difficult and will take some trial and error to fine tune your procedural generation algorithm.

29 / TACTICS: SQUAD FORMATIONS

Formation behavior help to create team cohesion on the battlefield and enhances the realism of combat. Formations are greatly used in games that involve large military battles and aerial dogfights.

FORMATIONS
LINE FORMATION - POSITIONING EXAMPLE

INDEX 0	INDEX 1	INDEX 2	INDEX 3	INDEX 4
AGENT	AGENT	AGENT	AGENT	AGENT

FIRST POSITION	DO: X + 5	DO: X + 10	DO: X + 15	DO: X + 20
INIT X = 0	X = 5	(5 x INDEX = 5 x 2)	X = 15	X = 20
		X = 10		

BASIC PROCEDURE:
ASSUME YOU WANT AGENTS IN A LINE, SEPARATED
EVENLY BY 5 UNITS.

1) START AT X POSITION = 0.
2) FOR EACH AGENT IN SQUAD, CREATE A WAYPOINT.
THE POSITION OF THIS WAYPOINT
WILL HAVE 5's ADDED TO ITS X VALUE DEPENDING ON ITS POSITION.
3) MOVE THE AGENT TO THIS WAYPOINT POSITION.

FORMATIONS
COLUMN FORMATION - POSITIONING EXAMPLE

FIRST POSITION

INIT X = 0
INIT Z = 0

AGENT

AGENT

DO: Z - 5

Z = -5

AGENT

DO: Z - 10

Z = -10

AGENT

DO: Z - 15

Z = -15

AGENT

DO: Z - 20

Z = -20

FORMATIONS
BOX FORMATION - POSITIONING EXAMPLE

FIRST POSITION

INIT X = 0
INIT Z = 0

AGENT

AGENT

DO: X + 5, Z + 0

X = 5
Z = 0

DO: X · 5, Z · 5

INIT X = ·5
INIT Z = ·5

AGENT

AGENT

DO: X + 5, Z · 5

INIT X = 5
INIT Z = ·5

FORMATIONS
DIAMOND FORMATION - POSITIONING EXAMPLE

FIRST POSITION

INIT X = 0
INIT Z = 0

AGENT

DO: X · 5, Z · 5

X = ·5
Z = ·5

AGENT

AGENT

DO: X + 5, Z · 5

X = 5
Z = ·5

AGENT

DO: X + 0, Z · 10

X = 0
Z = ·10

FORMATIONS
WEDGE FORMATION - POSITIONING EXAMPLE

FIRST POSITION

INIT X = 0
INIT Z = 0

AGENT

DO: X - 5, Z - 5

X = -5
Z = -5

AGENT

AGENT

DO: X + 5, Z - 5

X = 5
Z = -5

DO: X - 10, Z - 10

X = -10
Z = -10

AGENT

AGENT

DO: X + 10, Z - 10

X = 10
Z = -10

BASIC PROCEDURE:
ASSUME YOU WANT AGENTS IN WEDGE FORMATION,
SEPARATED EVENLY BY 5 UNITS

1) START AT X POSITION = 0, Z = 0.
2) FOR EACH AGENT IN SQUAD, CREATE A WAYPOINT.
THE POSITION OF THIS WAYPOINT
IF THIS POSITION IS RIGHT OF LEADER, ADD 5 TO X.
IF TO THE LEFT OF LEADER, SUBTRACT 5 FROM X.
THEN SUBTRACT 5 FROM Z (MOVING BACKWARDS)
3) MOVE THE AGENT TO THIS WAYPOINT POSITION.

30 / PROBABILITY-DRIVEN AGENTS

30.1 / SIMPLE ADAPTIVE AGENTS

In this chapter you will be introduced to the concept of a simple agent that can "adapt" to changes in environment and player gameplay styles. We are mainly concerned with an agent thought process that incorporates probability-driven learning. These days, game engine companies such as Unity3D are developing complex tools that utilize reinforcement learning and other machine learning techniques to power adaptive A.I. In your case, you should be focused on building a game with compelling A.I. characters – it is not necessary to dive into those complex subjects (of course, you are more than welcome to go to Unity3D.com and search for their machine learning capabilities).

In our simpler A.I. designs, we present a system that stores data on environment events and player actions, then make decisions based on the probability of such events. For example, if a human player hits his target only 15% of the time, the A.I. can deduce that its opponent has horrible shot accuracy or probably just started learning the game. Based on this data, the A.I. can decide to engage the human player using ranged weapons only, because ranged weapons and low accuracy are his areas of weakness.

An agent with adaptive capabilities can decide its actions based on previously learned data from events, objects, and the actions of the player or other agents. In other words, such an agent *adapts* itself by changing its tactics, preferences, and actions over time. Again, this is accomplished by collecting data during gameplay, training the agent using that data, and processing the data to determine a correct course of action. The chances of successfully selecting a correct action is positively correlated with the size of the dataset.

30.2 /   IS THIS "REAL A.I."?

In our opinion, probability-driven agents applied to video games are not complex enough to be considered as "real A.I.". We repeat: as game developer, you should be concerned with building the *illusion* that a computer opponent is intelligent, and minimally concerned with building "real" A.I. Another reason for avoiding the development of "real" A.I. is runtime performance concerns on your end-users' hardware and development speed.

30.3 /   WHY USE PROBABILITY-DRIVEN A.I.?

An agent that can learn and adapt during gameplay processes a plethora of data at runtime and makes myriad calculations based on that data. Combine these processes with the main game logic, advanced graphics processing (sprites, 3D models, shadows, anti aliasing, post-process effects, global illumination, etc), receiving player controller input, audio processing, special effects, physics engine processes, and more, your players' CPUs can be significantly overworked, resulting in slow and laggy gameplay. In most cases, using actual machine learning algorithms and neural network implementations to process the data is impractical from a gameplay performance standpoint, and unnecessarily time-consuming from a developer's standpoint. As a result, we prefer to employ implementations that simply give the illusion that the agent can learn.

Furthermore, as this book strives to empower even total beginners to design virtual characters, we will be using simple adaptive implementations powered by probability and a reward/punishment system to *simulate* an adaptive agent. You can understand how this works by analyzing the simple game of rock, paper, scissors. This simple system drives the agent's learning mechanism and force it to either perform or avoid a future action by checking the reward score of the previous similar action. Therefore, since we're dealing with simple numbers and an even simpler algorithm, you need not concern yourself with the complex theories or mechanisms behind real adaptive A.I. This chapter's focus is to present simple implementations of adaptive agents that can be employed by beginner developers using popular game engines, specifically Unity3D.

If, however, you are interested in exploring the actual concepts and implementations used in machine learning, you can start by researching up on the topics of "reinforcement learning" and "Q learning" which implements a system values that helps an agent to determine the optimal action, based on the consequences of a previously selected state and the consequences of the states selected after that.

30.4 /   ADAPTING IN ROCK, PAPER, SCISSORS

We can start to understand the concept of an adaptive agent by analyzing a very simple game: Rock, papers, scissors that pits a human against an AI opponent. Most of the time, the players of this game make random picks and outcomes are usually based on luck rather than strategy. But what if we can tip the chances of winning in the computer's favor, even if slightly? If the human player prefers to play "rock", it would make the game more challenging if the AI were to notice that and pick to counter that. Specifically, this computer opponent can accomplish this simply by recording the percentage of times the human player chose "rock", say, 90% of the time. On each turn, the computer opponent can look up this table of percentages and select "paper" with a 90% random chance in order to counter the human opponent. This type of simple logic can easily defeat a human player who has a preference for a particular pick, even if he changes his preference later. For example, the human player may prefer picking "rock" most of the time. After about 20 rounds where he had picked "rock" 12 times, the computer opponent may determine that the human enjoys picking "rock" and will pick "paper" to counter him. After a while, this human player may switch to preferring "scissors" instead of "rock". The computer opponent will notice this new trend and will respond accordingly.

But what if the human player does not have a preference for a particular pick? What if the he makes his picks purely based on what he feels the computer might pick next, based on the last pick? For example, the human player picks "rock" and loses when the computer picks "paper". Based on that, the human player might pick "scissors" the next round to counter that. The game developer here can take the analysis a step further, by having the computer opponent analyze, not only the percentage of "rock" being chosen, but also the *pattern* in which "rock" is being chosen. For example, the human player may pick "rock" 60% of the time *on the next turn*, after he had picked "scissors" the previous turn. The computer can then analyze the number of times the player picked "rock" after he had picked "scissors". Then, on the next turn, if the player had picked "scissors" the previous turn, the computer may have a high accuracy of predicting if the player will select "rock" next and act accordingly.

We can also reverse the analytical process so that instead of analyzing the human player's preferences, the computer opponent can analyze its own moves and predict whether a state or action will yield a positive or negative consequence. In this case, the game developer can define "states" for the A.I. Each pick, whether it be "rock", "paper", or "scissors", is a state. So when the A.I. opponent picks "paper" he enters the "paper" state. Each turn, the computer will enter a state which will yield either a consequence of "win" or "lose", depending on what the human player had picked. The game developer can set a base reward score for each consequence (win = 1, lose = -1). These numbers mean that the computer opponent is "rewarded" with a positive score on a good pick, and a negative score on a bad pick. At the end of each round, the following data is recorded into a lookup table: The computer opponent's pick and the reward score. After many rounds are played, the computer opponent will analyze this simple reward table for patterns that reveals the most and least successful picks. The computer opponent will then adjust his future picks according to this table.

This rock, paper, scissors example is simple and light on CPU because the computer opponent only has to consider 3 states: Rock, paper, and scissors, and 2 consequences (win or lose). In addition, it's easy for the agent to produce a large dataset in a short period of time, since each round usually lasts a few seconds. However, most games are not so simple. Consider chess, where the combination of every piece on a square is a state with many actions and the consequences of moving a particular piece to a particular square can branch out to a further 10 or more states, each with their own trees of consequences, eventually leading up to victory or defeat. Or consider a first person shooter game with computer opponents. To the computer player, there are many states to consider, each with varying consequences. The states here can include "Walk", "Run", "Jump", "Crouch", "Aim", "Shoot", "Dodge Left", "Dodge Right", "Run to Cover", and so forth. If the agent in this case were to be adaptive and gradually learn to be a better combatant, it must play enough rounds and store enough data to cover all the states, their outcomes, and the sequence of states and their outcomes. In this case, the game developer must take care that processing such complex datasets does not impact game performance for the players.

30.5 / ADAPTING VS CHEATING

This section's purpose is not to try to discourage you from using adaptive agents, but help you make better and more educated decisions in knowing *when* to implement one.

In game development, a key fact to remember is that the game developer, and therefore the game's A.I. system, always has full access to player and environment data. Given this, the game developer must decide whether to implement a simpler "cheating" system or an adaptive system where the A.I. that does not have prior knowledge of its environment and must gradually learn, or a combination of cheating and learning systems. In a cheating implementation, if an agent wishes to know where the human player is hiding, all it has to do is check the position of the player object. If the human player decides to switch his weapon from a pistol to a shotgun by pressing the number 2 key on his keyboard, the agent can receive this knowledge immediately, when the number 2 key event is triggered. If the agent wants to have perfect accuracy when shooting all it has to do is check the position of the human player and aim directly at it. Therefore, the agent never needs to "guess" where the human player is, what he's doing, or the exact position to aim at in order to hit him – it can simply look it up. This type of game A.I. system can be considered "cheating". Most games today use this type of agent because compared to adaptive agents, these are much simpler to implement and allows game developers to better fine-tune A.I. decisions. To simulate agents with varying skill levels, all the game developer has to do is inject randomness into an agent's actions. For example, to simulate an agent with an inaccurate aim, the game developer can simply add a small random number to a target's position, creating a new position nearby, and tell the agent to aim at this new position. This is an easy way to simulate inaccuracy and ensuring that the agent will miss the shot.

Let's revisit our rock, paper, scissors example. In our original design, we implemented a computer opponent that was "blind" to what the human player picked *before* picking either rock, paper, or scissors. This agent records what the player had already picked in the previous rounds and tries to determine an optimal counter pick based on that. But what if the agent was not blind to what the player picks? Let's assume that instead of using an adaptive agent, we simply cheated by making the agent decide a pick immediately *after* the human player picks. At the beginning of a round, 3 buttons show on the screen for the human player: Rock, Paper, and Scissors. As soon as the player clicks "Rock", the game runs through a list of rules (e.g. if PLAYER clicks ROCK, select PAPER) and immediately selects "Paper" in response. In this case, the agent did not ever need to consult a pre-recorded table of player data to guess what the player might pick next. The agent in this case cheated because the computer program always knew what the player picked. Thus, the agent here can play perfect games where it wins every single time. The game developer can decrease the difficulty level simply by adding a bit of randomness to the selection process. For example, instead of picking "Paper" every time the player selects "Rock", the agent can roll a random number between 0 and 1.0 inclusive. If he wants the agent to have a 30% chance of winning each round, he can create a condition that checks if the random number is between 0 and 0.3 inclusive. If so, the agent will pick "Paper", ensuring that the agent wins that round. If the random number is above 0.3, then the agent will pick anything but "Paper", ensuring either a draw or loss. Similarly, if the game developer wished to increase level of difficulty, he can simply increase the chance of selecting a winning pick (e.g. from 0.3 to 0.9 for 90%). As you can see, in this much simpler implementation of a rock, paper, scissors agent, no fancy calculations related to learning or adaptiveness were needed. If your goal was to create a simple rock, paper, scissors game with varying levels of difficulty, the choice between using this "cheating" method vs the adaptive agent method is clear. This same decision process applies to both simple and complex games. During your game's design phase, you must decide whether your agents really need adaptive behavior, or if implementing "cheating" behavior using a set of rules will easily suffice.

30.6 /   STORING LEARNED DATA

Simulating learning capabilities requires methods for storing temporary data at runtime and sometimes, permanently on disk. This data can contain events, Ids of states and actions, names of objects and players, probabilities, event outcomes, and more. The simplest way of storing this data at runtime is by using arrays or lists, both of which should be available to coders and non-coders in popular game development engines. For example, in Unity, C# programmers can use the built-in array system, C# lists or hashtables. Non-coders can use visual-coding tools like PlayMaker to visually build data structures using PlayMaker's own array implementation. For our example, we will be using C# arrays. More complex ways of storing learning data may include using XML, JSON, and embedding a database into the game, such as SQLite, MariaDB (an open source fork of MySQL). Be wary of some open source databases that restrict embedding into software for distribution. On desktop platforms, permanent disk storage is fairly straightforward. On mobile platforms such as the Android OS, you must consider user data storage permissions and the default file location for app data on a particular mobile system. On the HTML5 WebGL browser platform, developers should be able to use a browser's built-in web storage or in the small RAM space allotted to the browser, taking care to note the very limited storage space given to browser apps.

30.7 / DISCOVERING AND AVOIDING FIRE

Our example here examines a curious agent that is about to discover the dangers of fire. An object named "Fire" has been placed into our game scene. This object has an attached script that deducts the health of any agent that comes into contact with it. Our agent begins by first approaching this unknown "Fire" object. When he collides the fire object, a script on the object triggers a function that deducts a certain number from the agent's health. Afterwards, the agent stores into his memory a log entry containing the foreign object's name, the location of contact, the resulting event (health was lowered), and encounter statistics. The agent will log the total number of encounters and the number of encounters in which he was injured. Over time, the agent will combine this data into a "danger rating", and use it to predict that future encounters with the "fire" object will result in injuries and learn that such objects must be avoided. The following diagrams illustrate this example's events, known as "rounds." Each "round" represents an encounter with the fire object during which new data is logged.

(See diagram on next page)

ROUND 1

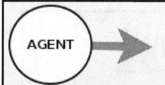

UNKNOWN OBJECT
OBJECT NAME: "FIRE"
DANGER RATING: ?
POSITION: (6, 5, 15)

TOUCH FIRE!
>> EVENT TRIGGERED!
{SUBTRACTED 50 FROM HEALTH}

ADD A NEW ENTRY INTO MEMORY WITH THE FOLLOWING DATA:

OBJECT NAME = "FIRE"   TOTAL ENCOUNTERS: 1
DANGER RATING: 20   TOTAL ENCOUNTERS THAT HURT ME: 1
LOCATION: VECTOR (6, 5, 15)   % OF DANGEROUS ENCOUNTERS: 100%

ROUND 2

 **KNOWN OBJECT**
OBJECT NAME: "FIRE"
DANGER RATING: 20
POSITION: (6, 5, 15)

EVENT TRIGGERED!
{SUBTRACTED 50 FROM HEALTH}

UPDATE EXISTING ENTRY WITH NEW DATA:

OBJECT NAME = "FIRE"	TOTAL ENCOUNTERS: 2
DANGER RATING: 40	TOTAL ENCOUNTERS THAT HURT ME: 2
LOCATION: VECTOR (6, 5, 15)	% OF DANGEROUS ENCOUNTERS: 100%

ROUND 3

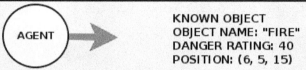

KNOWN OBJECT
OBJECT NAME: "FIRE"
DANGER RATING: 40
POSITION: (6, 5, 15)

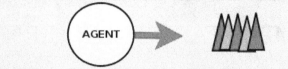

EVENT TRIGGERED!
{SUBTRACTED 50 FROM HEALTH}

UPDATE EXISTING ENTRY WITH NEW DATA:
OBJECT NAME = "FIRE"   TOTAL ENCOUNTERS: 3
DANGER RATING: 60   TOTAL ENCOUNTERS THAT HURT ME: 3
LOCATION: VECTOR (6, 5, 15)   % OF DANGEROUS ENCOUNTERS: 100%

ROUND 4

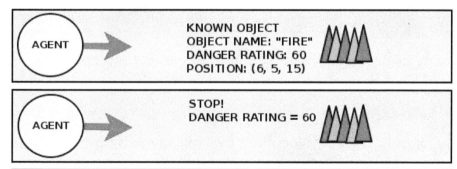

KNOWN OBJECT
OBJECT NAME: "FIRE"
DANGER RATING: 60
POSITION: (6, 5, 15)

STOP!
DANGER RATING = 60

AVOID AND PICK
NEW PATH

As you can see, the agent in the above diagrams repeatedly moves into the fire, hurting himself. At round 3, the percentage of dangerous encounters is still at 100%, meaning that 100% of the time the agent touched the fire object, his health dropped. Moreover the "danger rating" has increased by 20 every time the agent is injured. At round 4, the agent will refer to the statistics, checks that the fire object has thus far yielded a 100% injury rate, and proceeds to avoid the fire this time around.

30.8 /   SIMPLE TARGET PATTERN ANALYSIS

Often a human player's movements can be predicted, especially in a multi-area building or dungeon-like setting. Human players tend to develop preferences over time, especially if the same map or arena is played repeatedly. If you've played any of the popular online multiplayer shooter games such as Call of Duty, Halo, or Battlefield, then you're aware that human players tend to hide in a preferred area or "camp a location" as they call it. These preferences can be exploited to the A.I.'s tactical benefit. For example, consider a team deathmatch shooter game that takes place inside a house. The gameplay works like this: There is a game "map" consisting of a large house. In this house are clearly marked zones by the developer, such as "Kitchen", "Basement", "Yard", and so forth. Two teams spawn inside a random location in this house and compete for the highest score for their team by causing as much damage as possible through shooting or melee combat. Each time a player is killed, he respawns and the kill is added to the enemy team's score. The team with the highest kill score in 30 minute time span wins. An A.I. agent in this game can keep a log of the player's preferred locations by simply recording his vector positions and the zone he is in (e.g., "Kitchen area").

With enough data, the agent can use probability to predict where the player will most likely to go. For instance, if, across the entire duration of the game thus far, the player visited the garage 80% of the time, then the agent can hide in the garage 80% of the time to ambush the player. To grant a probability weight to certain room zones for an agent, simply feed a list of zones into the agent, attach a dynamic probability to each zone (in this case, 0.8 out of 1.0 is given to the garage zone), and have the agent randomly select a zone to move to, taking into account the probability of that zone. The next 2 diagrams illustrate the tracking of a player throughout this map.

(See diagram on next page)

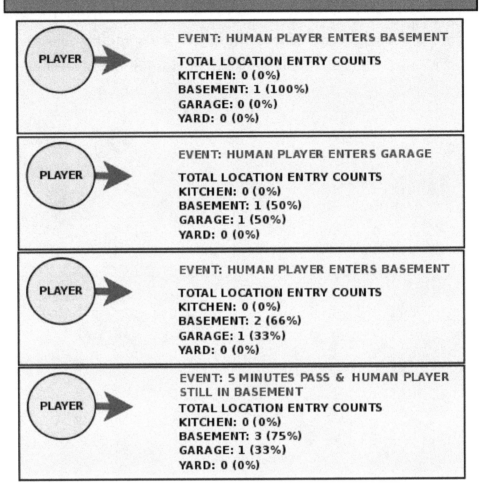

ROUND 1: LEARNING THE HUMAN PLAYER'S TRAVEL STYLE
(ALL EVENTS WITHIN 10 MINUTES OF GAME TIME)

PLAYER →

EVENT: HUMAN PLAYER ENTERS BASEMENT

TOTAL LOCATION ENTRY COUNTS
KITCHEN: 0 (0%)
BASEMENT: 1 (100%)
GARAGE: 0 (0%)
YARD: 0 (0%)

PLAYER →

EVENT: HUMAN PLAYER ENTERS GARAGE

TOTAL LOCATION ENTRY COUNTS
KITCHEN: 0 (0%)
BASEMENT: 1 (50%)
GARAGE: 1 (50%)
YARD: 0 (0%)

PLAYER →

EVENT: HUMAN PLAYER ENTERS BASEMENT

TOTAL LOCATION ENTRY COUNTS
KITCHEN: 0 (0%)
BASEMENT: 2 (66%)
GARAGE: 1 (33%)
YARD: 0 (0%)

PLAYER →

EVENT: 5 MINUTES PASS & HUMAN PLAYER
STILL IN BASEMENT
TOTAL LOCATION ENTRY COUNTS
KITCHEN: 0 (0%)
BASEMENT: 3 (75%)
GARAGE: 1 (33%)
YARD: 0 (0%)

Through 10 minutes of game time, it has been determined that the player has visited the basement area 75% of the time. At this time, a confrontation-inclined agent may choose to also move to the basement area 75% of the time. On the other hand, an agent that prefers to avoid combat may instead *avoid* the basement area 75% of the time.

The agent can use the data gathered to execute a decision tree similar to this:

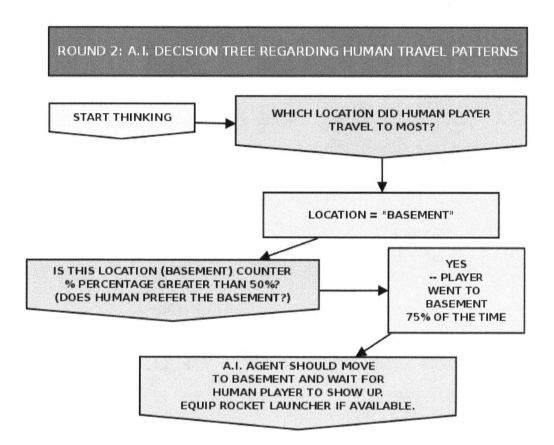

30.9 /   ADAPTING TO ENEMY COMBAT STYLE

The same concepts can be employed when predicting a player's combat style, such as his weapon choice and aiming. In this third example, a human player and an A.I. agent battle it out in a deathmatch game that features 3 weapon types: Fire, Water, and Ice. Fire weapons defeat ice, ice weapons defeat water, and water weapons defeat fire. Both players have access to all weapon types and selects a weapon when he spawns on the battlefield. Each time a player is killed, he is respawned again and has the chance to select a different weapon. During the course of the match, the human player repeatedly kills the A.I. agent, hitting him places such as the head, arms, legs, etc... Here is where our simple adaptive implementation comes in. Each time he is killed, the A.I. agent logs the weapon that the player used to kill him with and the location on his body that was hit. Over time, the A.I. agent can use this data to predict what weapon type the player prefers and the body area the player likes to shoot at most. Ultimately, based on the probabilities, the agent will on purposely select weapons that are the weaknesses of the player's preferred weapons, and purchase body armor for the body areas the player targets most. The following diagrams show the entire agent's adaptive process, from gathering player data to drawing inferences, to making a decision based on that inference.

(See diagram on next page)

ROUND 1: LEARNING HUMAN PLAYER'S COMBAT STYLE

EVENT: HUMAN PLAYER KILLS A.I. AGENT
HUMAN PLAYER USED WEAPON: FIRE
HUMAN PLAYER TARGETED: HEAD

TOTAL WEAPONS USE COUNT
FIRE: 1 (100%)
WATER: 0
ICE: 0

TOTAL TARGETED AREAS COUNT
HEAD: 1 (100%)
ARMS: 0
LEGS: 0

EVENT: HUMAN PLAYER KILLS A.I. AGENT
HUMAN PLAYER USED WEAPON: FIRE
HUMAN PLAYER TARGETED: HEAD

TOTAL WEAPONS USE COUNT
FIRE: 2 (100%)
WATER: 0
ICE: 0

TOTAL TARGETED AREAS COUNT
HEAD: 2 (100%)
ARMS: 0
LEGS: 0

EVENT: HUMAN PLAYER KILLS A.I. AGENT
HUMAN PLAYER USED WEAPON: ICE
HUMAN PLAYER TARGETED: ARMS

TOTAL WEAPONS USE COUNT
FIRE: 2 (66%)
WATER: 0 (0%)
ICE: 1 (33%)

TOTAL TARGETED AREAS COUNT
HEAD: 2 (66%)
ARMS: 1 (33%)
LEGS: 0 (0%)

EVENT: HUMAN PLAYER KILLS A.I. AGENT
HUMAN PLAYER USED WEAPON: FIRE
HUMAN PLAYER TARGETED: HEAD

TOTAL WEAPONS USE COUNT
FIRE: 3 (75%)
WATER: 0
ICE: 1 (25%)

TOTAL TARGETED AREAS COUNT
HEAD: 3 (75%)
ARMS: 1 (25%)
LEGS: 0 (0%)

ROUND 2: CONCLUSIONS ABOUT PLAYER'S COMBAT STYLE

TOTAL WEAPONS USE COUNT
FIRE: 3 (75%)
WATER: 0
ICE: 1 (25%)

TOTAL TARGETED AREAS COUNT
HEAD: 3 (75%)
ARMS: 1 (25%)
LEGS: 0 (0%)

OBVIOUSLY IN AN ACTUAL GAME, THERE WILL BE MANY MORE
DATA POINTS (HUNDREDS) ABOUT THE HUMAN PLAYER'S TACTICS
BUT FOR THIS EXAMPLE, WE WILL ONLY USE A SMALL SET.

FROM THIS DATA, WE CAN SEE THAT THE HUMAN PLAYER PREFERS
USING FIRE WEAPONS 75% OF THE TIME, AND ICE WEAPONS 25%
TO KILL HIS TARGETS. ADDITIONALLY, HE PREFERS TO AIM
AT THE HEAD (75%), AND SOMETIMES AT THE ARMS (25%)

ROUND 3: A.I. AGENT ADAPTS TO HUMAN PLAYER'S STYLE

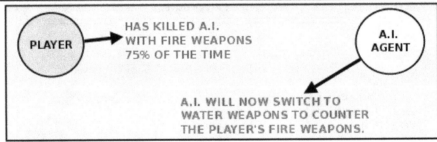

PLAYER — HAS KILLED A.I. WITH FIRE WEAPONS 75% OF THE TIME — A.I. AGENT

A.I. WILL NOW SWITCH TO
WATER WEAPONS TO COUNTER
THE PLAYER'S FIRE WEAPONS.

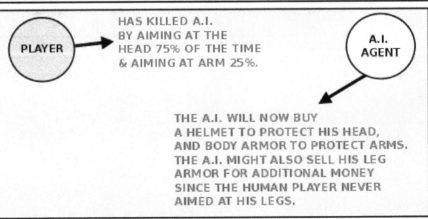

PLAYER — HAS KILLED A.I. BY AIMING AT THE HEAD 75% OF THE TIME & AIMING AT ARM 25%. — A.I. AGENT

THE A.I. WILL NOW BUY
A HELMET TO PROTECT HIS HEAD,
AND BODY ARMOR TO PROTECT ARMS.
THE A.I. MIGHT ALSO SELL HIS LEG
ARMOR FOR ADDITIONAL MONEY
SINCE THE HUMAN PLAYER NEVER
AIMED AT HIS LEGS.

30.10 /   TAMING A WILD ANIMAL

In this final example, a dog companion agent proceeds cautiously towards the human player before becoming tamed and friendly. Here, a simple adaptive A.I. procedure creates a "friend rating" on the human player from the actions taken by him towards the dog.

(See diagram on next page)

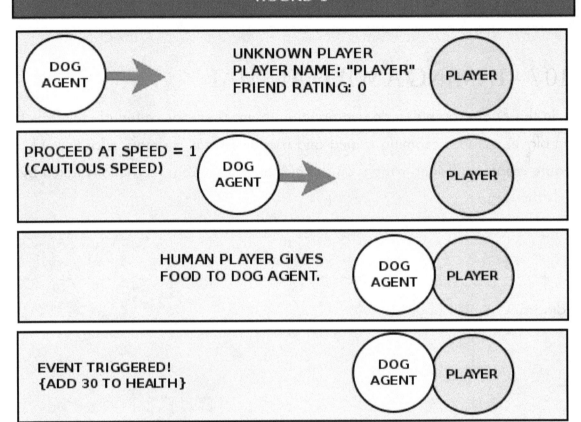

ROUND 1

DOG AGENT →

UNKNOWN PLAYER
PLAYER NAME: "PLAYER"
FRIEND RATING: 0

PLAYER

PROCEED AT SPEED = 1
(CAUTIOUS SPEED)

DOG AGENT → **PLAYER**

HUMAN PLAYER GIVES
FOOD TO DOG AGENT.

DOG AGENT **PLAYER**

EVENT TRIGGERED!
{ADD 30 TO HEALTH}

DOG AGENT **PLAYER**

ADD A NEW ENTRY INTO MEMORY WITH THE FOLLOWING DATA:
PLAYER NAME = "PLAYER"   TOTAL ENCOUNTERS: 1
FRIEND RATING: 20   TOTAL ENCOUNTERS THAT HELPED ME: 1
                               % OF FRIENDLY ENCOUNTERS: 100%

ROUND 2

KNOWN PLAYER
PLAYER NAME: "PLAYER"
FRIEND RATING: 20

PLAYER

PROCEED AT SPEED = 2
(NORMAL SPEED)

PLAYER

HUMAN PLAYER GIVES
FOOD TO DOG AGENT.

DOG AGENT   PLAYER

EVENT TRIGGERED!
{ADD 30 TO HEALTH}

DOG AGENT   PLAYER

ADD A NEW ENTRY INTO MEMORY WITH THE FOLLOWING DATA:
PLAYER NAME = "PLAYER"   TOTAL ENCOUNTERS: 2
FRIEND RATING: 40   TOTAL ENCOUNTERS THAT HELPED ME: 2
                               % OF FRIENDLY ENCOUNTERS: 100%

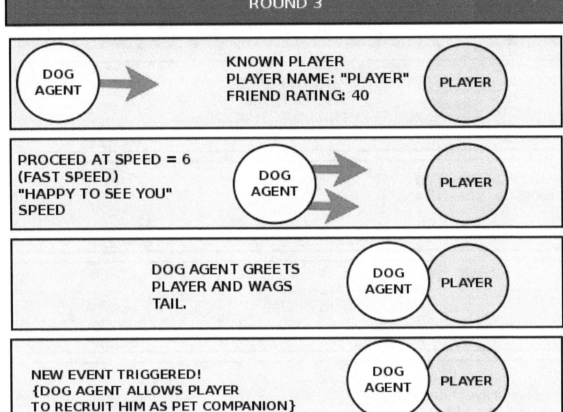

ROUND 3

DOG AGENT →

KNOWN PLAYER
PLAYER NAME: "PLAYER"
FRIEND RATING: 40

PLAYER

PROCEED AT SPEED = 6
(FAST SPEED)
"HAPPY TO SEE YOU"
SPEED

DOG AGENT

PLAYER

DOG AGENT GREETS
PLAYER AND WAGS
TAIL.

DOG AGENT

PLAYER

NEW EVENT TRIGGERED!
{DOG AGENT ALLOWS PLAYER
TO RECRUIT HIM AS PET COMPANION}

DOG AGENT

PLAYER

31 / COMPANION AGENTS

A companion character is a broad term used to describe any agent that accompanies the human player. Such a character can be a tamed pet, squad member, wild animal, quest companion, or more.

Companion agents that follow the player should constantly scan and move within a radial zone around the player. In simple implementations, companion agents can simply follow the exact same path as the player, by way of virtual "footprints" saved in memory. Such footprints are actually waypoints created across time, at the player's current position. For more realistic implementations, such as a companion in a complex RPG, the developer should first define a radius around the player (follow distance) and move the companion to a random location inside this radius. Such an implementation is similar to target stalking tactics and if have already developed code for target stalking, you can simply duplicate or share the functions of your script for use in companion following.

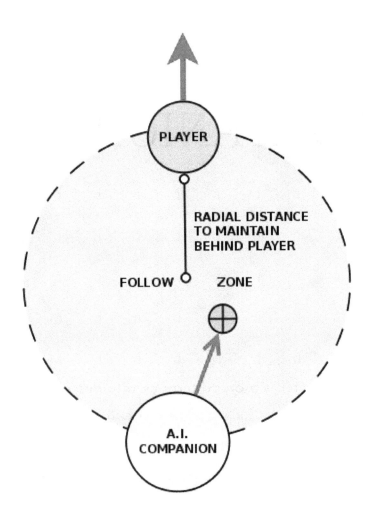

32 / INTRODUCTION TO FINITE STATE MACHINES

A term often used in game development is "finite state machine" or "FSM". At the basic level, an FSM is simply a model for organizing a finite number of states where an entity can only be in one state at any given time. In an FSM, *events* are triggered by *conditions* and an entity moves between states using *transitions*. FSMs can be used for a plethora of development activities, such as powering game logic, playing animations, receiving user input, and A.I. agents. Finite state machines are an important topic in game A.I. because they provide a straightforward method for designing, developing, and debugging agents. Additionally, most popular game engines provide tools for developing an entire game, A.I. included, using finite state machines, aimed at artists without any programming experience. Therefore, whether you decide to use FSMs to develop your A.I. or not, it's beneficial to become familiar with them.

The FSM model can be used to implement both simple and complex A.I. characters. An example of a simple implementation is an agent powered by an FSM using only two states: *Guard* and *Attack*. The agent begins at the default Guard state and continuously scans the nearby area for hostile objects. When a hostile object is detected, the agent transitions from the Guard state to the Attack state. During the Attack state, an attack animation is played and damage is deducted from the target's health. The Attack state then continuously checks if the target is alive or terminated. If the target terminated, the Attack state transitions back to the Guard state and the cycle begins again.

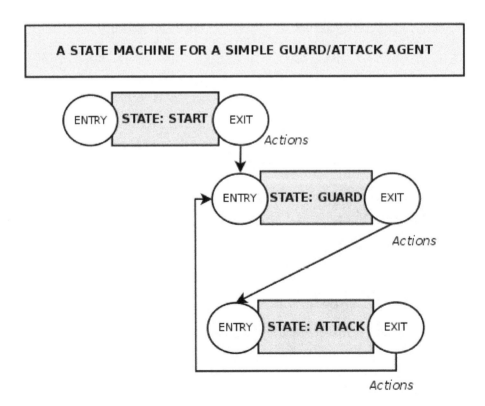

A benefit of the FSM model is that the game developer can modify agent behavior by inserting new states without affecting the older ones. Continuing our example, we can make our agent more interesting by adding a new state between the Guard and Attack states called "Chase". The agent's behavior is now modified when the Guard state detects a hostile object. Instead of triggering attack mechanisms, the agent will now pursue the target to get within a specified range before transitioning over to the Attack state.

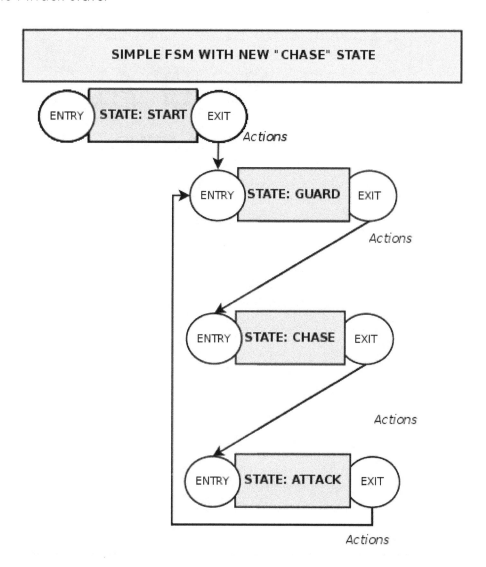

33 / THE BRAIN MODULE: PUTTING IT ALL TOGETHER

A central, core module is needed to unify all other modules in order to simulate a believable virtual agent. We can this central module the "Brain". This brain module should contain the underlying logic that helps to define the A.I. agent and can be readily swapped out with another brain module if needed. It has access to all global functions of the other modules, specifically the Sensory, movement, and combat modules. It constantly gathers the data collected by the Sensory module, makes decisions, and relays commands to the movement, combat and other modules to execute actions.

The brain module can be implemented using either coding and non-coding techniques. Programatically, the brain module can be implemented using a single *class* of code that accesses sensory data either in real time or at predetermined game ticks, and calls the global functions of the other modules, also represented by classes. Most popular game engines support development workflows that do not involve any programming at all. For developers taking the non-coding route, the brain module can be implemented in a similar fashion as the programming method. For example, some game engines come with tools to build finite state machines without using any coding. Every module can be represented by a collection of states and decision trees. The collection of states that represent the brain module can simply transition out to the entry states of the other modules.

The following diagram shows a simple brain module that implements a decision tree to simulate an intelligent agent:

(See diagram on next page)

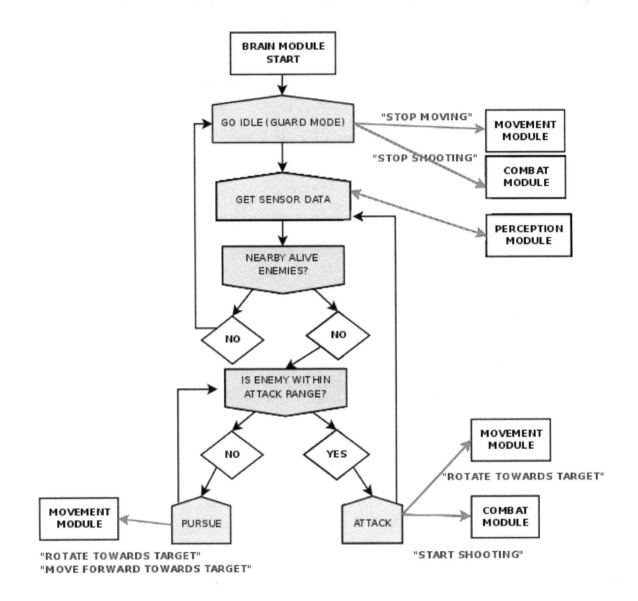

In this brain module, the agent begins at the default *Idle* or *Guard* state. It queries the Perception Module for data about its nearby environment. This includes retrieving the positions of every enemy object in the game scene and checking the distance from each enemy to itself. If an enemy is both within its sight range and alive, then it moves onto the next phase: Pursue or Attack. To decide between chasing the target and attacking it, the agent simply checks whether the distance between the target and itself is within its attack range. If so, it triggers a "Rotate" function in the Movement Module to rotate towards the target and a "Shoot" function in the Combat

Module to begin firing projectiles. If the target is not within attack range, then the agent will enter the Pursue state which will trigger both a "Rotate" and "Move Forward" function in the Movement Module. This will cause the agent to rotate towards the target and move forward at the same time. If the Movement Module is employing a pathfinding system, then a minor adjustment must be made to the Pursue phase as it must now wait for the pathfinder to calculate a viable path to the target before continuing. If no viable path is found, then the Pursue state must transition back to the Guard state, restarting the cycle.

It is usually not good practice to run brain module logic in absolute real time for performance reasons. Rather, decision logic should be run at specified intervals (e.g. that give 0.3 seconds) to give the illusion of real time thinking. In Unity, this means that the code for the brain module usually should not be placed inside the *Update()* or *FixedUpdate()* methods. It is an inefficient use of your player's CPU when an agent is constantly running scans and conditional checks in the background, even when it is outside the action zone. This inefficiency is multiplied by magnitudes in large battle scenes. A simple and fast way to implement this is to use Unity's *InvokeRepeating*. An example follows:

```
public class AIBrain {

    public float thinkInterval = 0.3f;   // 0.3 seconds


    void Start(){
            // InvokeRepeating(function name, start time, repeat time);
            InvokeRepeating("Think", thinkInterval, thinkInterval);
    }


    void Think(){
            // insert A.I. brain logic here
    }


}
```

34 / EXAMPLE CASES

34.1 /   FIRST PERSON SHOOTERS

All tactics and concepts used in this book can be applied to first person shooters. First person perspective games have become very common these days, but that does not change the fact that the "first person" experience is still a unique experience, one that often seeks maximum realism. Furthermore, with the increasing popularity of virtual reality headsets and the more powerful machines they can run on, first person games can be both an immensely satisfying gaming experience for players, and a major source of revenue for game developers.

Many first person shooters attempt to create a soldier experience, combat seen through the eyes of a soldier on the battlefield. As such, the A.I. used in first person games must be able to convince the player that he is either collaborating with or fighting real people or creatures. Tactics, combat, dialogue, and a fluid movement system become critical elements to first person shooter A.I.

If you are developing a first person shooter, especially a commercial game to compete in the current market, you should aim to accomplish one or more of the following:

1. Cover system for A.I. agents – they should dynamically find cover behind walls and under objects

2. Dialogue & agent interaction – Character interaction with the player is almost a requirement these days, especially in single player games. A.I. agents should have multiple dialogue options and voice acting if possible. If you are an indie developer with a low budget, you may ask a few friends to record a few sentences for you – anything is maximize the immersion that is expected of a first person game.

3. A.I. tactics such as flanking, stalking, stealth, and formations.

34.2 / RACING GAMES

In a racing game, the primary objective for an agent is to defeat all opponents by having the best time in moving through a track. Using our modular A.I. system, we can simulate racing vehicles such as cars and aircraft, or animal racing such as horses and people using waypoints. The same concepts apply to 2D and 3D racing games.

Consider the following race track:

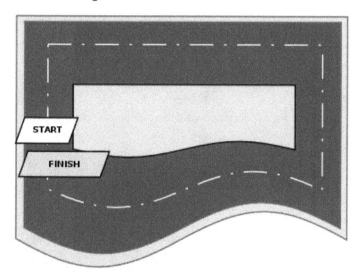

A level designer would place waypoints at all corners, curves, and bends on the track for an A.I. agent to follow:

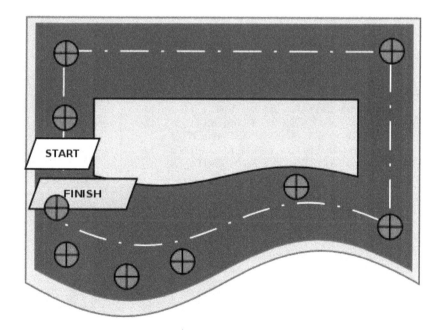

At runtime, an agent will simply utilize our waypoint system to drive through each waypoint in the series:

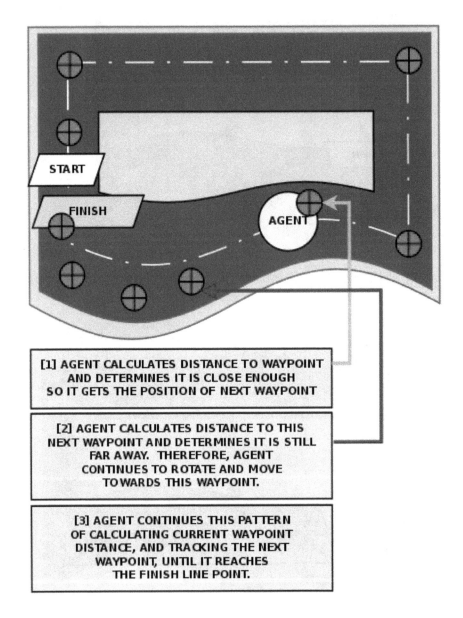

To simulate agents (racecar drivers) of varying driving abilities, speed, and car performance, the developer can randomize the speed and turning rate of an agent as he approaches the next waypoint. For example, an "easy" racecar opponent may have a random speed between 10 and 20 while a "tough" opponent may have a random speed between 20 and 50.

34.3 /   TOWER DEFENSE

In a tower defense-type game, the player must place turrets at strategic locations at the beginning of each level in hopes that he will defeat the incoming enemy wave by using his turrets. Such a game will utilize 2 types of agents that share the modules we covered: turret agents and moving enemy agents.

Turret agents are simply combat agents with a partial movement module in that there is no movement ability, only rotational capabilities. A turret agent's combat module will have ranged attacks that partially cover the battleground and utilize a variety of weaponry and projectiles.

Enemy agents in this case become simplified combat agents, with a movement module that can process waypoint and an optional combat module (in some popular tower defense games, the enemy agents can shoot back at turrets, but this is usually not the case).

In the following diagram, immobile turrets are placed at the center of the game map, able to shoot at incoming enemies. When an enemy wave begins, enemy agents will follow the waypoint system (waypoints in red). This waypoint movement system is similar to the race car track shown in the previous chapter.

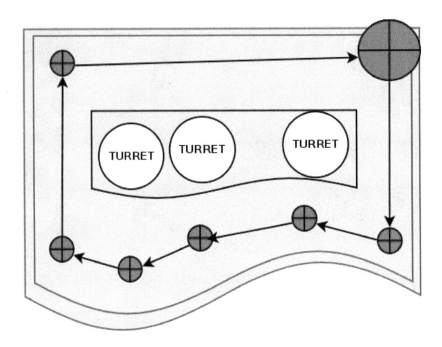

34.4 /   SOLVED GAMES

In a solved game, the outcome can usually be predicted based on players' current positions. "Solved" refers to the fact that such a game has a finite number of moves and counter-moves that can be predetermined. Solved games are usually unrelated to A.I. characters and, unless you are developing a board, card, or puzzle game, you most likely will not run into the need to develop A.I. for such games. However, it's still important to know what they are as solved games are quite prevalent in certain game genres.

A famous example of an easily solved game is tic-tac-toe. In tic-tac-toe, the A.I. can potentially play perfectly, with a counter-move for every position, either claiming victory every time, or forcing the player into a draw. If you are building a tic-tac-toe type game, decision trees can be instrumental in helping the A.I. to decide its next move. For example, you can always begin by playing the center or corner square. After the player moves, the A.I. can run through a decision tree, checking the player's move and providing a counter position.

Some games can be "partially-solved". An example of a partially-solved game is chess. To date, no A.I. chess engine has been able to analyze and predetermine every single possible move and combination of moves on a chess board. Perhaps such a feat is possible in chess games that have significantly reduced pieces or squares.

If you're interested in exploring this area further, here are a few important concepts that you should study:

- Minimax algorithm

- Game trees

- Combinatorial game theory

- Game theory & the concept of perfect play

- Zero-sum game

- Non-probabilistic decision theory

34.5 / SPORTS GAMES

Finite state machines and decision trees are a perfect match for A.I. in sports games. Athletes on a team in real life have specific roles at any given point during the game, and, depending on the sport, such roles can be reversed with the players on another team. These same real life roles are analogous to the states in a finite state machine in a virtual game.

Consider a hockey game, where two teams of players compete to score the most goals. Each player on a team at any given time has either an offensive or defensive state. When a team scores a goal, the puck is passed to the opposing team and the roles are reversed. The next diagram shows an example agent in a hockey game that has both offensive and defensive capabilities.

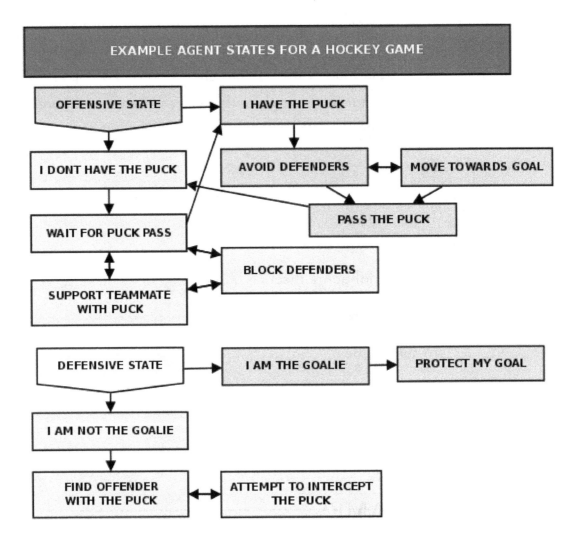

35 / ABOUT THE AUTHOR

Rui Jiang wants to empower people of all ages and experience levels to build captivating games that entertain, educate, and enliven people's lives. Rui developed the *GAME AI MADE EASY* series to significantly simplify the knowledge and technical expertise required to build compelling characters that lead to a great game. His ultimate purpose is to to help aspiring game developers to achieve their creative dreams by minimizing or eliminating altogether, technical barriers.

Rui has over 15 years of technical experience across a wide spectrum of technologies and platforms and has been involved in long term development of many AAA privately-funded projects, such as the animated film series Memoirs of a Warrior and Next Universe. In addition, Rui has developed A.I. systems for the Unity game engine that have gone on to become best sellers on the Unity Asset Store, such as AI Designer Pro and Population Engine. Rui has been fascinated with A.I. ever since he picked up his first game as a kid in the 1990s. Inspired, Rui spent his early childhood teaching himself to code on his mom's Pentium 133, programming primitive games, and hasn't stopped coding ever since. He has studied at George Mason University and Columbia University.

36 / INDEX

Alphabetical Index

37 / **NOTES**

www.ingramcontent.com/pod-product-compliance
Lightning Source LLC
Chambersburg PA
CBHW060532060326
40690CB00017B/3469